THE
TRANSFORMING
BELIEVER

THE TRANSFORMING BELIEVER

ZULIBE TURNER

authorHOUSE®

AuthorHouse™
1663 Liberty Drive
Bloomington, IN 47403
www.authorhouse.com
Phone: 1-800-839-8640

Published by AuthorHouse   12/20/2012

ISBN: 978-1-4772-5108-9 (sc)
ISBN: 978-1-4772-5109-6 (e)

Books of the Bible and Their Abbreviations

Old Testament New Testament

Genesis—	Gen	Matthew—	Mt
Exodus—	Ex	Mark—	Mk
Leviticus—	Lev	Luck—	Lk
Numbers—	Num	John—	Jn
Deuteronomy—	Dt	Acts—	Ac
Joshua—	Josh	Romans—	Rom
Judges—	Jud	1 Corinthians—	1 Cor
1 Samuel—	1 Sam	2 Corinthians—	2 Cor
2 Samuel—	2 Sam	Galatians—	Gal
1 Chronicles—	1 Chron	Ephesians—	Eph
		Philippians—	Phil

2 Chronicle—	2 Chron	Colossians—	Col
Nehemiah—	Neh	1 Timothy—	1 Tim
Psalms—	Ps	2 Timothy—	2 Tim
Proverbs—	Prov	Titus—	Tit
Ecclesiastes—	Ecc	Hebrews—	Heb
Isaiah—	Is	1 Peter—	1 Pet
Jeremiah—	Jer	2 Peter—	2 Pet
Ezekiel—	Ez	1 John—	1 Jn
Daniel—	Dan	2 John—	2 Jn
Hosea—	Hos	3 John—	3 Jn
Amos—	Am	Jude—	Jud
Micah—	Mic	Revelation—	Rev
Nahum—	Nah		
Habakkuk—	Hab		
Zephaniah—	Zeph		
Haggai—	Hagg		
Zechariah—	Zech		
Malachi—	Mal		

Dedication

To my two beautiful daughters: Princess-Esther and Precious; my dear youngest brother Joshua who is turning into a fine young man and my nieces and nephews. I have prayed that the Lord will cause them to know Him and that they will accept Jesus as their Lord and Saviour. And, when this time comes that they will receive the understanding of the revelation of the power of Jesus Christ.

For Prayer Request, Please Contact the author:

Email: tfaith95@yahoo.co.uk

Acknowledgements

My immediate family especially my husband Howard Ogbonmwan, parents, my brothers and sisters who stood by me in my most trialling times and gave me love and support with embracement of kindness when I needed one. May you receive the special grace of God to run the race of life and at the end of your journey on earth make it to heaven in Jesus name! God bless you.

Memory Verses (NIV)

John 3:16

For God so loved the world that he gave his one and only son that whoever believes in him shall not perish but have eternal life.

Joshua 1:8

Keep this Book of the Law always on your lips; meditate on it day and night, so that you may be careful to do everything written in it. Then you will be prosperous and successful.

Luke 1:37

For no word from God will ever fail."

Matthew 18:18

Truly, I tell you, whatever, you bind on earth will be bound in heaven, and whatever you loose on earth will be loosed in heaven.

Matthew 7:7

Ask, and it will be given to you; seek, and you will find; knock, and the door will be opened to you. For everyone who asks receives; he who seeks finds; and to him who knocks, the door will be opened.

Isaiah 1:18

"Come now, let us settle the matter", says the Lord. Though your sins are like scarlet, they shall be as white as snow; though they are red as crimson, they shall be like wool.

Psalm 8:4

What is humankind that you are mindful of them, human beings that you care for him?

Jeremiah 29:11

For I know the plans I have for you," declares the Lord, "plans to prosper you and not to harm you, plans to give you hope and a future.

Palm 8:2

Through the praise of children and infants, you have established a stronghold against your enemies, to silence the foe and the avenger.

CONTENTS

Preface

In this era of economic crisis and the increase of wickedness in a hopeless world, where all the theories of the world's leader are failing, hope comes to us in the light of our Saviour Jesus Christ. He came from heaven and died on the cross, was risen on the third day, ascended into heaven, and will come again to take His own to everlasting life. My desire is to tell as many people, as possible willing to hear about this Jesus and His saving power. He is the ancient of days, yet, the bright morning star.

This book will enlighten your understanding of your calling as a Christian. It will encourage and motivate you to press on to the very end of your lifetime whilst walking with Jesus. It will give you confidence in God and cause your faith to more the hill to a new ground.

Having said that, God's love for the human race has truly inspired the author to such an extent that, His faithfulness towards me, is so extraordinarily mysterious that, there are the feelings of incompleteness inside of me if I withheld my testimonies hence,

I am obliged to tell someone about Jesus. I pray that others people who will read this book will enjoy such goodness I found in Jesus.

May the grace of our Lord Jesus Christ and, the fellowship of the Holy Spirit be with you now and forevermore Amen!

The Vision: A Personal Discovery

As a young teenage, the author was attracted to a bible that was lying around in her parent's bedroom. On one momentous day, she picked the bible up and to her surprise, she discovered, it was a birthday gift presented to her by her parent, on her fifth birthday.

She was concerned about the reason for her parent to choose a bible for her fifth birthday's gift. With so much courage began a line of enquiry. The response was very shocking, when the mother broke the good news that, Zulibe passion for biblical stories was so great and extraordinarily powerful that, she could read and memorise some of the psalms at that age. Exceptionally, her preference for a song when asked to do a miming was a Christian song.

It was almost certain, that the parent saw something special about her and so they bought the bible to encourage her with the things of God.

The author also believes within her that, it was a divine act of God. She said that, the beauty of the stars, the sunset, the moon, the falling rain, gardening and nature were some of the most passionate events in her life. From a young age, the author hold very closely to her heart that, there was something beyond our natural life but just did not know what it was, until she found the amazing Jesus.

By the time she became born again Christian, full of great passion for the things of God, the Lord reveal Himself to her in dreams.

During this teenage years, though, she was not completely sure whether she was dreaming or awake, but she knew, what was happening to her was AN ACT OF God SHOWING her a vision which was to come.

However, before she gave her life to Jesus, she has dreamt of events or of people and things that eventually, happened in the natural life

The mother was worried about all those dreams she had from time to time as a result, the mother cautioned her not to disclose to other persons. She feared she would be harm.

The Author Perspective

In one of my vision, I saw myself in a field when suddenly I looked up the cloud and I saw Jesus coming down from above the cloud. On one side of Jesus was Moses and the other side was Elijah.

No one told me who those people I saw were. Something in my spirit knew who they were. They were dressed in brown sack garment. Jesus came down very closely to me and shows me his hands; he said, see this is the hole I bored for you when I was, crucified on the cross. He gave me a hugged while Moses and Elijah stood by him, one in the left and the other in the right. Jesus hugged was very compassionate and gentle. I could see he is holy and full of love.

I saw Moses holding something like the tablet of the Ten Commandments as they depart from me into the clouds but when I looked closely at the item that, mosses held in his hand, it was the book 'Isaiah' that was boldly inscribed on it. The tablet was the last thing I saw held in the hands of Moses and soon they disappeared into the clouds.

Following that dream, I began to read the book of Isaiah, to my surprise I found out that this book of Isaiah is one of the most powerful book of the bible. Isaiah as a man is often referred, to as **"The Messianic Prophet"**, because, of his many prophecies that were fulfilled in Jesus. The New Testament quotes and applies more scriptures from the book of Isaiah than any other Old Testament prophet applies.

In the book of Isaiah the prophet, prophesy about the birth and the crucifixion of Jesus Christ respectively. It further tells us the importance and significant of the crucifixion of Jesus to the world.

I believe I am call to preach the gospel of Jesus to humanity. I am therefore, privileged for God to give me this opportunity to write this book to tell someone about this saving power of Jesus. I pray, that as many as could give their life to Jesus, because of this book of personal testimonies, they will receive the knowledge of the power of the resurrection of Christ Jesus.

In another dream, I saw myself in this same field but this time, it was a mourning of a dead child. Everybody was crying and weeping and I saw myself telling the people that Jesus can raise the dead and I walked towards this child's coffin. I prayed for her in Jesus name, and then asked her to get up in the name of Jesus. She got up and I gave her to her parent. I have not rose the dead but I have twice in the Gambia and Reading UK respectively been in a position were a girl and a woman had collapsed on the floor.

Both cases are very similar, they both stretch and became stiff, eyes rolling and helpless and seem dying. At that point, I had boldness and something strongly told me to lay my hands on them and pray. They both sudden become able and the first thing they asked for was water to drink but could not explain exactly what had happen to them. All they said I only hard you prayed in the name of Jesus. But, I knew that voice which I heard internally, was the spirit of God and the power of his resurrection witnessing silently to me at that moment.

I must tell you that, the devil had tried everything to stop me from reaching you, but God has a plan for his entire children and these plans according to Jeremiah 29:11 is good and not evil and to give us a future. I have in many ways tried to evade the responsibility God has given me, however the ministers of God had always find a way to fish me out no matter how hard I tried. In all this, I have learnt a lesson in that; it is not about me, but all about Jesus. Today, as I set down to write this book, I say the devil has failed woefully. For he who has begun his good work in me is able to finish it. Thank you, Jesus loves you.

Introduction

Being Born Again

To 'be born again' is a significant appeal of our Lord Jesus Christ to all people of the world. It is the start of a living spirited relationship with Christ Jesus and spiritual lightening of our path with greater opportunities and new challenges met to prepare us for a greater responsibility with God.

Alternatively, it is a transforming process from the deadliest and frightening darkness both within our hearts—minds and from the existing boundaries, that preoccupies our hearts and minds including the misperception of the world around us to an amazing light that brightens our lives beyond worldliness' of the human nature.

Being born again connotes a new spirited life for a new believer. The experience of being born again signals the sowing of a heavenly and spiritually cleansing seed into a profound fertile foundation or soil.

By nurturing of the seed; providing it with the right supplements, (the word of God and keeping the right association) the sower (new believer) create the opportunity for the seed to germinate and grows into a new shape, characteristics and culture which bears resemblance of the works and spirit of Jesus Christ.

'To Believe in Christ Jesus' is spiritually self-transforming process.

'Born Again' is a sudden spiritual awakening and self-rediscovering, which happens by the expression of our internal faith, to align with the acceptance of Christ as our personal redeemer. Thus walking our faith in Christ in a spiritual eternity contract with the Lord Jesus, to such effect that, we accept—that Jesus had truly offered himself onto us as living sacrifices for the cleansing of our sins and indeed knowingly, it is an unmerited favour received of or from Christ Jesus. Accordingly, John said "And this is the record, that **God** hath given to us eternal **life**, and this **life** is in his Son" (1John 5:11). The favour to receive from God, comes of the grace of God at a point we decided to trust the son of God—Jesus Christ with everything about us and give Christ the fullest leadership over our lives (1John 1:5-10; 1John 2:17).

This commitment brings about special physical manifestation in our lives. This spiritual encounter with Christ generally transformed us like an erupting volcano. It marks for us an upward journey in a vertical spiritual direction. The spiritual vertical journey works in phases or stages. This begins as a babe believer doing listening whilst been consistently nurturing milk from the Word of God, to a serious adult believer (a doer of the Word by putting the faith to test through the leap of faith in the Word of God) with profound encounter with the Lord Jesus Christ, our author and the finisher of our faith.

It is by the leap of our faith in Christ we begin 'the will of God,' that which brings the transformation that will eventually change our lives in a dramatic way. This leap of faith in Christ Jesus is the core and the soul of the actionable Word of God. It makes God get motivated and gets God's attention towards us together. It inspires Christ abundantly and sufficiently to trust to work with us. Taken together, faith wins for us the heart and mind of God, allowing God

THE TRANSFORMING BELIEVER

to be present in whatever we do, joining his arm in ours to the extent that, God can extend our own future in order to fulfil our destiny.

God can erase and re-write whatever that has been wrongly said against us to our favour and success See the book of Isaiah and the message to king Hezekiah.

Accordingly, the Scripture write, 'Without faith it is impossible to please God' (Hebrews 11:6). The outcome of the leap of the faith in Christ is the demonstration of the Christ-like living and the way of life, we immediately and continually formed after our first encounter with Christ. It is the new way of we form with Christ that leads to an external life in Christ Jesus. On the other hand, in the natural environment, the new way of life put a light to the path of all those around us whom bear witnesses to our transforming lives by our works, including helping us to project the true characters of God's children (1 Peter 2:9).

God, Grant Us a Choice and Free Will

The Lord grants each one of us equal opportunity and free will to seek after the things we want, knock by faith, and ask with the hope we can receive. He made declarations after declarations and promised to be faithful until the end, even when we remain unfaithful.

He gave us a choice and advised us why He wanted us to be satisfied with this choice (Gen 2:16-18). He allows us to engage our mind and our hearts to search our imagination and beyond our apprehension to find solution, even if, he knew that there are bumps on the road and by given too much, we may become complacent about whether he exists at all, yet the Lord is unrestrictive of our free will. This is amazing! Each of us as human being has this freedom of choice: A choice to choose between good and evil. This is the amassing love of God.

Whereas, He allows us the freedom, He knew also that, we are not the architects of our lives and there would come a time that the structural foundation of our lives could become unstable if, we chose the wrongful direction because, of our creed and the love of self and worldly things.

He also knew by being "the omnipotent and omnipresence nature or God that we will require the creator (architect of all creations) to fix the faults embedded within our lives and bad behaviours. These include faults beyond the common eyes or understanding and fault that pastors, specialists, or world-renowned experts can never permanently affords us solutions.

These behaviours or and wrongful choices we made at some points in our lives including, failing in love of neighbourliness relationship, failing to obey God calling, friendship with wrong crowd, drunkenness, prostitution, failing forgiveness, committing fraud, witch-hunting, and living in crime.

These hotspots in our lives, wherein God intervene, to show Himself are the beginning of a new future for us especially set aside for us as a turning point. Perhaps, to enable us crave the understanding of the inner calling hidden within us by God.

A special moment, destined to be exploited or evolve at a very radioactive time in our lives, because, God, intends to demonstrate its sovereignty and set a full reconciliation with us—(forming new covenant that erases permanently all faults, sins including guilt we hold against God and those around us which at different point in our lives threaten our existence).

These periods of dwelling with the faults, enables us to see the reality of our lives, in phases: our fear, our unreasonable resistance, our breaking point, brownout or burn out seasons, successes, our joy, our hope, and our failure, above all, who we are, where we are from, and where we are heading.

The only reason we encounter these moments is to test our free will, our judgement of all the things we have achieve, things we know and things we pretend to know, and things we know that we shall never know. These include the discovery by Adam and Eve of their nakedness and finding their breaches of trust (Ephesians 1:9-11).

The Silent Listener and Patient Waiter

These sensitive times of our lives are when God knocks on our doors then He has a moment wait for our reactions and our actions.

Whether, it occurs to us to listen to the 'Word' and obey the Word of God. in particular, given the invisible sensation within us signalling power beyond our control or by the virtual breaking news about our lives, or by the pronouncement of some strange effect to impact upon our lives which to all circumstances, we hold the belief about the existence of 'unknown forces' at work.

I said '*unknown forces*' because; we are still struggling to recognise God.

Moreover, we arc not conscious of the knowledge of his Word. We are still struggling to accept change and accept that Jesus Christ is come and he's about to testify about his presence in our lives, all of the times but our selfishness rendered him inactive in our works.

Even though, he may never be part of the judgement and our decision that brings us to the moment we are in (remember the freewill principle of greater love granted to us). This is where God shows up and shows his spirit as the only supreme authority (one and absolute authority) and He shows his spirit is in control and has come to take control of what He started when he agreed to form us and bring us into this world (Mathew 28:18; John 14:6).

In other words, he predestined us for a purpose (Proverb 21:30); this also reminds us of the Scripture. In John 3:16, Jesus Christ emphatically stated, 'For God so loved the world that he gave his one and only Son, that whoever believes in him shall not perish but have eternal life.' In addition, in (Isaiah 9:6) the Bible proclaimed him as Wonderful, Counsellor, The Mighty God, The Everlasting Father, and The Prince of Peace.

God Affects All: Meeting of the Hearts and Minds

Geographically, it is at such a dangerous momentous time in our lives that the Lord opens our sub consciousness, our hearts, and minds towards free reasoning and the search to rediscover ourselves, in particular, to discover who is actually in control of our lives.

This meeting point between us on one hand and God (the creator) on the other side, the author liken to the location where 'two plates meet,' which geologists call a *plate boundary*. Plate boundaries are commonly associated with geological events, such as earthquakes and the creation of topographic features like mountains, volcanoes, mid-ocean ridges, and oceanic trenches (Wikipedia viewed 25/10/2012 about 22:48).

This illustration of geological events constitute the most fearful things of nature of which are all the creations of God or happens as act of God, whereas the spiritual projection of the power of God is a personal encounter with Christ Jesus. A spiritual plate boundary defines the momentous meeting between a human being and God in his infinite authority. When this takes place, it signals the battle of the hearts and minds. It witnesses the connection between every organ of the body to form into one most powerful union manifesting the power of God intricately linked to the spirit of God. At which stage, we are spiritually consumed by the Holy Ghost fire and reconciled with God in a spiritual recreation of our hearts and mind (Ephesians 1:10; Ephesians 2:14; Ephesians 2:16). Please, see also John 14:8-10.

A spiritual plate boundary in other words, is the instantaneous transformation in our spirit to receive Christ as our Lord and personal Saviour. This is when the content of our hearts and minds are instantaneously defeated. By the pouring of new spirit, to fill the vacuum left in the sudden excavation, (cleansing by the blood of Jesus), which successfully occurred at the momentous opportunity that the spirit of our Lord Jesus Christ descended upon us, and eventually our lives never remain as they were before the meeting. Any individual who has truly encountered Jesus Christ will testify. Even friends and family around them, or more so the public (community), can bear witness of the transformation of his or her renewed spirit with a complete positive attitude towards life in general and the community in particular, professing overwhelming love of God over everything around him or in a very honest way.

God can transform you in a very exceptional way. God can make your lowland into a mountain, your valley to a sea, your sea to dry ground, and the shackles around you to be broken—breaking into total freedom beyond exceedingly and abundantly what you always wanted. God returns beyond where you hope you could have been. He compensates you including the times of your failures, the period of your defeats and in particular, beyond the events you were never aware existed because, you were spiritually blindfolded.

The Power of God Is Sufficient to Free Us of All Sins

Because of the greater power in Christ, like the 'biological diffusion process,' he instantaneously, displaces faster than the speed of light 'the prince of the world' from our hearts and minds setting us free indeed.

God cleansed by his blood. God renewed and recreate in us: a new heart, mind, and spirit. God does these things, before He comes into our lives and occupies the vacuum left vacant for which the egocentric authority or adventurer's spirit of 'the prince of the world' has once occupied or has illegally dominated in our lives due to excessive abuse of our acclaimed 'free will' or 'choice' (1 Peter 5:8). This is why the Scripture told us, 'And Jesus said, somebody has touched me: for I perceive that power has gone out of me.'

This spiritual transition or cleansing, from sins, which instantaneously takes place inside us signals territorial reclaim and occupation of the spirit of God, with greater legitimacy, and according us spiritual personal sovereignty. This is referred to by the reassurance in the Scripture: "You are of God, little children, and have overcome them: because greater is he that is in you, than he that is in the world" KJV (1 John 4:4).

It is a magical moment wherefore; we appreciated as baby Christians ascending from our faith to our calling, a calling that will help us align ourselves with the purposes we were predestine by God, the author and the finisher of our faith.

Decision! Decision! Decision!

It takes just a moment judgement and decision for the spiritual process to complete. This takes such reorganisation in form of a spiritual displacement following which we come to a firm and just decision. A decision we feel very strongly proud about for which is difficult for other people around us to understand precisely why we will take such a stance and what we mean when we say on occasions that something powerful is been lifted off us. We feel at peace with ourselves, then we become very much at peace with our environment, even more so with our enemies—those who will dislike us because of our new nature and declaration that Jesus is Lord (John 15:19). This is because that which has been displaced is replaced by the renewal of our hearts and minds just as new as an infant babe whose parent(God) hold a responsibility to protect (Roman 16:20; Luke 10:19) but only different by the very food we are recommended to eat.

We are present with a menu of the Word of God—the 'Bible' the book of life that reflect and contain our culture that will edify our body and mind. This is the prescription we feed our hunger and taste. The word of God is the nutrient we feed to grow as a young Christian believer.

The menu contains directions that will increase our faith by the words we speak and the companions we continue to associate ourselves.

The Scripture tells us that, as will obey God's Word, who shall be against us (Romans 8:31-39).

Significantly, by the time we made the declaration of accepting the Lord Jesus Christ as our personal Saviour, we are spiritually, lifted up and above all circumstances of things unseen and discernible and whether thrones, powers, rulers, or authorities, because, God created everything. Moreover, the bible tells us that, at the mention of the name of Jesus everything shall bow down and worship Him.

Again, we are continually, guided by the scripture, our faith without ceasing reaffirming our trust at all times in Gods hand KJV (Psalms 27:1-3; Deuteronomy 33:29).

Our New Life Begins Here!
Proudly Walking with God

This new position we occupy signal a new beginning for us to have or feel the fullness of the glory of God in our lives to the effect that, the Holy Spirit empowers us with increasing faith to pronounce with such boldness that, we have become born again.

Because, we have undergone the spirituality to be born out of the cleansing blood of Jesus Christ with the benefits to accede to our title as children of God as mentioned earlier in (1 Peter 2:9).

The biblical authority, according to (1John 5:4), definitely, within us, we have the sudden feelings of security, internal cleansing, and strong feelings of spiritual transformation and excitement to walk with God.

In addition, by the renewal of hearts and minds, we come to form the internal knowledge of newer feelings, which feeds our attitudes in spiritually sensitive ways. This feeling deep inside our hearts and minds eventually affect positive behaviours that make us easily distinguishable, spiritually and physically manifested in the agape love which are seen amongst those Christ believers or 'born again' (Matthew 7:20; and 7: 24).

Chapter 1

What Does It Mean To Be 'Born Again'— Encounter with Nicodemus.

In John 3:1-21, we read the story of Nicodemus, a certain man who came to Jesus by night to ask, 'How can a man be born again?' This man Nicodemus got the answer to eternal life in seeking. This confirms that in our seeking of the truth with God, we will always find the answers to our questions.

John 3:1-6wrote: Now there was a man of the Pharisees named Nicodemus, a member of the Jewish ruling council. He came to Jesus at night and said, 'Rabbi, we know you are a teacher who has come from God. For no one could perform the miraculous signs you are doing if God were not with him.' In reply, Jesus declared, 'I tell you the truth; no one can see the kingdom of God unless he is born again.' How can a man be born when he is old? Nicodemus asked. 'Surely he cannot enter a second time into his mother to be born!' Jesus answered, 'I tell you the truth, no one can enter the kingdom of God unless he is born of water and the spirit. Flesh gives birth to flesh, but the Spirit gives birth to Spirit.'

Nicodemus was a Pharisee and a member of the Jewish ruling council, which means that he was well recognized and highly respected in his society. He was also an educated man, an expert on the law. You will naturally expect someone like Nicodemus to know it all. The Bible was his field of study. Just think about it: the Pharisees used to write the Scriptures on their forehead. They were proud of their knowledge. Given their expertise in the disciplined, they still could not recognize the identity of Christ or how can one get salvation. Nevertheless, the Bible tells us that Nicodemus came to Jesus by night to ask, 'How can a man be born again?' Personally, I believe that for a man as Nicodemus to come to Jesus and to come at night, he must have thought about it thoroughly and pondered on this for some time. He must have come to the point where he had to acknowledge of the truth of Jesus's teachings and that Jesus himself was all knowing.

With all his education and intellect, Nicodemus could not get an answer to his own question but needed an answer. He also must have believed and been persuaded that Jesus is of the Lord and the only one that will give the correct answer to his question. This is why Nicodemus referred to Jesus as 'Rabbi,' meaning 'teacher,' and said 'we know.' He came humbly to seek answers from the one whom had proved to be greater teacher than he was. This shows you can read the Bible and still not know whom God is. To know God, you need to go beyond just reading, it takes the power of the Holy Spirit.

We see that in Jesus's reply to Nicodemus's question, he said, 'No one can enter the kingdom of God unless he is born of water and spirit. Flesh gives birth to flesh, but the Spirit gives birth to the Spirit.' Jesus talked about the kingdom and the Spirit. This is because in order for you to understand the revelation of 'born again,' you must consider the following facts in life:

o   How and why where you created and born into this world?

o   The effects of 'being born again'.

The Answer
How and Why Were You Created and Born into This World?

In the beginning, when God created the heavens and the earth, he also created man. Now God is a Spirit and has no body. The Bible tells us in Genesis 2:7 that after God formed man from the dust of the ground, he breathed into the nostrils of man the breath of life and the man became a living being. God breathed his Spirit into man and man became alive. This is the very breath of *God*. Now we know that man is a spirit living in a body as a human or living being.

After God made man he took man and put him in the Garden of Eden so that man can work it and take care of it and to have dominion over all God's creations. However, God commanded man not to eat of the tree of good and evil. 'You are free to eat from any tree in the garden; but you must not eat from the tree of the knowledge of good and evil, for when you eat of it you will surely die' (Genesis 2:15-17). God created us and not of our own. Now we learnt that in the beginning, when God created the world, he also created man. 'So God created man in His own image; in the image of God He created him; male and female He created them' (Genesis 1:27).

Disconnected from God's Plan

The Bible tells us in Genesis 3, that after the creation of Adam and Eve, they were tempted, by the serpent—the Devil to eat from the tree of the 'knowledge of good and evil.' In that incident, the Devil said craftily, 'You will not surely die' (Genesis 3:4). Yes, their mortal bodies did not die instantly, but their eyes became open and they became conscious about what is good and what is evil (Genesis 3:6, 7). Their bodies began to respond to the nature of the world. Instantaneously, their bodies began dying. This assertion of death described how the spiritual and emotional relationship between Adam and Eve and God ended. A new but distance relationship was formed between God and the human Race. God created humans with good intentions, however, our disobedient made us to become distance from God because, God, is holy, truth and spirit, which

3

bear no relationship with sin. Therefore, God annulled the original contract with the human kind. He then created a new one that allows humans to find for themselves beyond the Garden of full provision of all social—economic needs.

God gave Adam and Eve dominion over all his creation and to fellowship and have a relationship with God. However, God in his glory cannot accommodate sin. It is impossible for sin to dwell in the presence of God. Their disobedience to adhere to the temptation of the Devil also caused them separation with God. It also vexed God that man had chosen to disobey and sin against him; he felt it so much that the Bible tells us in the book of Genesis that God regretted he made man.

God had to remove Adam and Eve from the Garden of Eden because of sin. This was an inevitable act of God because sin and holiness cannot live together. God is holy and has no sin in him. The glory of his holiness cannot accommodate sin. Nevertheless, God loved man; it is the will of God to have relationship with man. God never made man to die. He did not intend man to be sick or have any form of ailment. Rather it was an act of love. He wanted man to enjoy and rule all his creation.

This love of God for man is so profound that He causes God to have compassion for Adam and Eve even though they chose to sin against him. Therefore, God made the first sacrifice for man by killing an animal to make garments for Adam and Eve and clothe them to cover their nakedness and sin. However, this did not stop them from dying—as the blood of an animal is not worthy or powerful enough to cleanse the sins of man. God did not send them naked out of the garden. What an awesome God we serve.

Even in our greatest disobedience, God still love us. When you invite God to come into your life, you are inviting God to cover your nakedness and recognise him as your Lord and Saviour.

The Effect of Being Born Again

Man lost his place in God in the Garden of Eden. Man became exile, separated from God. The only way that man could be reconciled to or with God was through spirited sacrifice. This has to be one of an imperishable blood. We saw in the whole of the Old Testament how man made all kinds of sacrifices in order to reconcile to God and make atonement for sin.

However, these sacrifices only covered their sins and never purified or cleanse the sins of man. This is because; the blood of cows and bulls is not holy or powerful enough to cleanse the blood of man. This blood has to be superior and without sin or blemish. Therefore, the only way is through God himself. No blood of man or angels is fit to cleanse the blood and sins of man except that of God.

God therefore, sent down his only begotten son—the man Jesus (God the son). God came to earth as a form of man who is Jesus to die for our sins. Jesus is the Emmanuel, spoken about, in the book of Isaiah, meaning 'God with us.' It was prophesied by Isaiah in Isaiah 9:6-7 that a child is to be born and 'his name shall be called Wonderful, Counsellor, Mighty God, Everlasting Father, Prince of Peace . . .' These prophesies were fulfilled in John 1:1, 2, and 14. 'In the beginning was the Word, and the Word was with God and the Word was God.' In verse 14, the Word became flesh and dwelt among men. This Word is the man Jesus, whom the prophet spoke of in the Old Testament.

The Reconciliation with God

Human beings are or were separated from God because, of sin. God, however, sent Jesus to die for our sins so that, through the blood of Jesus we can be reconciled back to God. This is why we need to be born again. You cannot reconcile with God through your righteous works; it is only through Jesus. The Bible tells us in Isaiah 64:6 that all our righteous works are like filthy rags before God.

In 1Peter 1:3, he said, 'Praise, be to the God and Father of our Lord Jesus Christ! In his great mercy, he has given us new birth into a living hope through the resurrection of Jesus Christ from the dead and into an inheritance, which can never perish, spoil, or fade.'

The Bible also tells us that, there was no one worthy of breaking the seals and opening the scroll that was in the right hand of God. There was no one in the whole of the heavens, on earth, or under the earth, and there was no one worthy of redeeming the world from sin, death, and eternal damnation except the lion of the tribe of Judah, the root of David. Revelation says, 'You are worthy to take the scroll and to open its seals, because, you were slain, and with your blood, you purchased men for God from every tribe and language and people and nation. You have made them to be a kingdom and priests to serve our God and they will reign on the earth' (Rev 5:9-10).

We see that just as sin entered into the world through one man (Adam). **Through one-man call, Jesus, the blood Jesus shed on the cross, bought our sins, (redeemed us) before he then reconciled us with God.**

Romans 3:23 wrote: 'All have sinned and fall short of the glory of God'. Therefore, no living person can ever say, I have no sin. We all have sinned and were born into sin, hence, we cannot redeem ourselves; this is why we need Jesus. It is a good decision to accept Jesus as your Lord and Saviour in your life. It is a decision that will never fail you, and your life will never be the same. It does not matter what status you hold, how and what you think of yourself and what picture other paint of your characters. No one who comes to the King of Kings will go back the same. There is bound to be a change in the life of that person. Yes, in sin we were conceived and born because of the sin that was passed on from Adam, the 'father of mankind,' to us from heredity and from generation to generation.

If you were to trace your root, you will end up at Adam and Eve home. This is why the blood of man does not choose the colour, status, gender, tribe, or from which part of the world you are. We are all children of Adam.

In Isaiah 1:18, God said, 'Come now let us reason together, says the Lord. Though your sins are like scarlet, they shall be as white as snow; though they are red as crimson, they shall be like wool.' God sent his only Son to die for our sins so you can be saved and have everlasting life. The Bible tells us in John 3:16, 'For God so loved the world that he gave his only begotten son, that whosoever believed in him should not perish but have everlasting life.' Amen.

When one is 'saved,' he/she has been born again, spiritually renewed, and is now a child of God by right of new birth. He or she now has a personal relationship with Jesus Christ and is trusting in Jesus Christ, the One who paid the penalty of sin when He died on the cross. This is what it means to be born again spiritually. 'Therefore, if any man be in Christ, he is a new creation' (2Corinthians 5:17). Because, the incorruptible blood of Jesus bought us, we became the righteousness of God through Christ and not of our own. Because of the blood of Jesus Christ, that you are saved.

Ephesians 2:8-9 wrote: 'For by grace you have been saved through faith and that not of yourselves; it is the gift of God, not of works lest any man should boast.' By grace you are saved and not by yourself. God promise is for everyone to become save. No one can boast of been saved by self-righteousness, but you can boast of the love of God for you.

The Bibles tell us that, now; there is no condemnation in Christ Jesus. We were restored, in our rightful place with Christ Jesus, because, he pays the price for us. This is how valuable you are. Therefore, never think less of whom you are. You are the righteousness of God. Praise the Lord!

In 1Peter 1:18-19, the bible said 'We were saved; we were redeemed and justify not of corruptible things but with the precious blood of Jesus.' The Bible refers to the highest possession and valuables of man as perishable. Things like gold and silver are referred, to as perishable items. Nevertheless, it is evident that the blood of Jesus is more valuable and precious than anything we can imagine or hold valuable. His blood is incorruptible.

7

Encounter with Jesus the Redeemer

When John the Baptise saw Jesus in the book of John 1:29, he said, 'Behold the Lamb of God that takes the sins of man.' Before Jesus came on earth, we were under slavery. The master of this world, the Devil, enslaved us through the disobedience of Adam and Eve. Adam sold his birthrights—to the Devil, by allowing the Devil to tempt him. A slave does not have any right over his own life. He cannot decide to do anything for himself without the consent of his master. A slave cannot one day decide that he wants to relax and enjoy the finest things on earth today, nor can he say, 'I don't want to work today.' He only does the will of his master.

A slave takes care of his master's business and does all the hard work on behalf of his master. A slave is therefore, a valuable asset to his slave master. In order for anyone to take a slave from his master, the slave would be purchased and with a price. Before another person purchases or redeems a slave, it must cost him/her something, because, that slave is useful to his master.

God saw Adam in slavery. He saw his generations to be born into slavery. This was not the will of God for Adam. God was not pleased with the position Adam had put himself in. God wants us to be free and enjoy freedom, so he pays the price and redeems us from slavery. He pays the price for us with the precious blood of Jesus.

'To redeem' means 'to pay back.' Jesus took back the birth right of Adam from the Devil and gave it back to Adam. Apart from the fact we were save and then redeemed by the precious blood of Jesus; the Devil cannot claim us, as his own, he cannot also enslave us anymore. The Devil's Authority is render powerless and when compared to a person, bought by the precious blood of Jesus, the Devil's authority is worthless.

For the above reason, the Devil cannot touch, tamper with you or and kill you, insofar; the Devil sees or find you are covered with the blood of Jesus. He cannot do you any harm, because you were bought, with the highest price—the highest price of Jesus, the holy one of God. The blood of Jesus is priceless, and it is also very costly and the most expensive thing you can ever receive. The Devil cannot touch you not because of your righteousness but because of the blood of Jesus. He knows that greater is he that is in you than he that is in the world. You are of great value to God, and it is not the will of God that, any man should perish. This is why it is necessary for you to give your life to Jesus, because you cannot save yourself. Take for example: the President of United States, the most important man around the world, because of the values of the people of United States project around the world. However, important he his cannot protect himself, his life in terms of safety rest upon God. In all things said, the United States confirmed this in the legal tender US Dollar that 'In God We Trust'.

Historically, the President of United States rely on the effort of his appointed local and international intelligence Agents: the CIA and the FBI to physically give him safety and security when he moves from one place to another, what he eat, whom he associate, and how he associate, when to travel, how he positioned as he meet and greet.

Even when he returned to his home, yet Agents on guard when he sleeps, he is never alone; they shed him like an Angel of God. Therefore, the spite is the President of United States; the President, does not has what it takes to protect himself from the viciousness of the enemies around. He sincerely and equivocally relies on the Agents goodwill or loyalty on oath and upon the covenant sown to, by the Agents whilst accepting the most important job they do which sometimes can cost their lives, have no recourse to justifies mistakes and negligence whether active or passive misjudgement whilst undermining the code of conduct. Moreover, when the President approved the rightful and trusted aid he just approved to put his life in their hands for adequate safeguard.

Similarly, you do not have what it takes to purchase yourself, but you have the right to choose where you want your soul to be when you die. You are extremely important and worth more than any gold or silver. When you chose to give your life to Jesus, you gave him the approval to save you from the slave master. Likewise, if you choose to be in control, you will consistently interferes with your destiny of which you have not expertise and adequate vision but just act on balance of probability. Then you ask yourself the question, it is excellent opinion to let the expert look after the things they are suited for and let God look after the things he created and known exceedingly better. Can a patient assist a Surgeon whilst under surgical knife? Let me leave you with this thought to meditate upon it.

The Journey to Spiritual Birth

The journey to be born again is spiritual. The expression *born again* means to be born of God and above all principalities, power, in high places including things known, heard, and perceived, seen and unseen. It does not matter whether; these things existed before man or in existence today. Born Again comes from having your faith tiled in God's hands together, becoming one with Christ Jesus.

For example, Nicodemus had a real need. He needed a change of his heart—a spiritual transformation or rebirth. Being born again is an act of God whereby: eternal life is pronounced and conferred upon a believer at the point of acceptance and the new believer's name is written in the book of life. *We believe by faith.* Hebrews 11:1 says 'Now faith is the substance of things hoped for, the evidence of things not seen.' The salvation of God is sure and it obtained as external life through Christ.

Accordingly, in the days of Moses, Moses sin against God, as a result could not make it to the Promised Land. Then upon Moses death, the devil came to collect the body and contended with archangel Michael claiming that, the body of Moses belong to him, in reliance of God's word that the wages of sin is death (Romans6:23) consequently, relying on Mathew 25:46 which said "Then they will go away to eternal punishment, but the righteous to eternal life."

Contending with the Devil, Angel Michael said to the Devil, 'the Lord rebukes you' (Jude1:9). Because, the Lord has promised that, He shall have mercy upon whom, he chooses to have mercy (Exodus33:19), this demonstrates the Power of the Blood of Jesus, our sole Defence Counsel before God the father, whereas, the devil the accuser in trial of Moses or sinners waiting to make you take the wrapped of condemnation (KJ Matthew 10:32).

The reason why we are required to believe in the salvation of God by faith is because; the kingdom of God does not function as we do on earth. It is a world where miracles, signs, and wonders are a way of life. You need the currency of faith to operate or work with the Word of God. Although, the Word of God can be proven, beyond any doubt, to be true, in giving your life to Jesus, you must believe by faith. The Bible says, 'But without faith it is impossible to please him for he that comes to God must believe that he is and that he is a rewarded of them that diligently seek him' (Hebrews 11:6).

You experience spiritual rebirth by accepting Jesus as your Lord and Saviour. The spirit of man is reconciled back to God. By being spiritually reborn, your spirit man can now relate with the spirit of God. It is only the spirit of a man, which knows the secret things of a man. Therefore, it is only the spirit of God, which knows the secret things of God. If you want to know of God's secrets and all his plans for you, you must learn to relate with the spirit of God. Nevertheless, the spirit of God is holy.

It is only when you give your life to Jesus that your spirit in you can be reborn. Your old spirit will be reborn through the blood of Jesus Christ. This new spirit is the spirit of God. Jesus promised us that he would, never leave us or forsake us. For this reason, even when he left us and went to heaven, he sent down the Holy Spirit of God. Remember, Jesus is God with us in the flesh. Now we have the Holy Spirit who is God with us in the spirit. This Holy Spirit is our comforter until Jesus comes back for the church (Christians). This Holy Spirit, which is the spirit of God, will teach you all the secret things of God. The spirit of God is the greatest of them all (Zechariah4:6)

How Can a Man Be Born Again?

This is a decision any man can take; it is, however, by far the most important powerful decision any man can make in his life. Nicodemus wanted to have an answer to this question. In Christianity the answer to eternal life is by been born again through Jesus Christ. According to the scriptures, this is the only way one can enter in to the Kingdom of God. As our spirit cannot die, we are face with two choices in our decision-making.

- Accept Jesus as your Lord and Saviour and be saved. Save by the blood of Jesus and live with him in glory.

- Live in sin or self-righteousness and be condemned into eternal damnation.

There is a choice between eternal life through Christ or eternal damnation. There is no middle ground. The Word of God cannot change. The Bible tells us that everything will pass away, but the Word of God will never pass away. The Word of God will never change to suit any man or woman. It is forever settled. God's standard has not changed from the beginning of time to now. God is the beginning and the end. In Romans 10:9-10, it says if we confess with our mouth and believe in our heart, we shall be saved.

First, you have to believe by faith in your heart that Jesus is Lord, and then confess it with your mouth. This is the greatest faith a man can have. Faith in the existence of the Lord Jesus and his saving power for your life, and the greatest miracle is to be born again. When you become born again, you rightfully become a child of God. The Bibles says, 'But as many as received Him, to them He gave the right to become children of God, to those who believe on His name: who were born, not of blood, nor of the will of the flesh, nor of the will of man, but of God' (John 1:12-13).

Again, God saved us, not because of the righteous things we had done but because of his mercy. He saved us through the washing of his blood and by rebirth and renewal by the Holy Spirit, whom he poured out on us generously, through Jesus Christ our Saviour (Titus 3:5). The apostle Paul in Ephesians 2:1 says, 'And you He made alive, who were dead in trespasses and sins.' To the Romans in Romans 3:23, the apostle wrote, 'For all have sinned and come short of the glory of God.' Therefore, a person needs to be born again in order to have their sins forgiven and have a fulfilling relationship with God.

No one is too young or too old to be born again. Salvation is not for the poor or rich but for *whosoever* believes in the Lord and it is priceless. You do not have to pay for it. It will gain you everything and lose you nothing. The Bible tells us in Joel 2 that in the last days, God will pour out his sprit upon all flesh. God is not a respecter of persons. He is not interested in your sacrifices but your availability. If you can make the choice for him to come into your life, you will become his child.

There is no measure of sin that can stop God from receiving you as his child. When you call upon his name, he will come into your life and will make you a new person. My brethren, do not let anything stop you from accepting Jesus as your Lord and Saviour. The Bible tells us that it is better for you to go into heaven with one arm than to go into hell with two hands.

This is a decision you have to make for yourself. Salvation is now. Time is not on your side and Time, definitely, will not wait for you. If you are not born again and you are reading this book, please, know that, it is not by mistake that you have chosen to read this book. God has led you to this book so you can have your chance in meeting Him. Time waits for no body, and tomorrow is not a promised to anyone. This might be the very last time for you on earth. No one knows when exactly, he or she will die. This is why you ought to make this decision now. This might also be the decision that will make you to live another day. Accordingly, it is appointed unto man to die once. After this, it is judgement.

The book of Luke15:10 tell us "Likewise, I say unto you, there is joy in the presence of the angels of God over one sinner that repents".

Whatever your circumstances, this decision will change your destiny forever.

Living on the Sea Cliff

We are in the most trying period of all; Jesus can come at any time. What is stopping you from accepting Christ as your personal Lord and Saviour? Is it your husband or wife, or girlfriend or boyfriend, which is stopping you, or even your precious money, career, fame, or position? I want to let you know that, it is better for you to go to heaven with one arm than go to hell with two arms. God will take care of you and your needs. He has promised that if you seek him first and his righteousness, he will take care of your family and all your love ones. He will also supply and add all other things that you desire.

You do not have to wait until you get married and settle down and maybe have one or more children. Salvation is now. How can you tell if you will ever get marriage or have children? How do you know you will ever get old? There was a time in my life when my relationship with God deteriorated. I had no peace of mind; I worked in between two jobs and yet found myself broke at the end of the day. I tried to comfort myself in saying that I would wait until I get married then I would recommit myself wholly to God.

Guess what! I never got married. It was only when I repented while working in my own strength and asked God for his forgiveness, and made the decision to put God first in my life and above every other thing. This included cancelling my Sunday job and instead going to church on Sunday and worshiping God.

The process of changing my priority, putting God first and fellowshipping with him, my now husband and I suddenly realised that we had been engaged far too long! I had even lost my engagement ring over a year before I got marriage, but to my surprise, I suddenly found my engagement ring after I got married, without even looking for it. It was a miracle for me. I believe it is because I chose to put God first. God then looked at my heart and saw that my desire was to be married.

On the night of my wedding day, I thought and said if only I had been sensible in totally giving my life to him as my Lord and Saviour to trust him for every need of my life. Seek God first, and everything will be added to you.

It is very foolish for a man to pile up riches on earth only to then die as an unsaved man. This is worse than poverty. There will be no one to redeem you from eternal damnation. It is better to die a rich man and know that you will even be richer afterwards. This is profitable. You cannot save yourself. The question is how can a man be saved?

In Galatians 5:19-, Paul identified the "works of the flesh" as "sexual immorality, impurity, depravity, idolatry, sorcery, hostilities, strife, jealousy, outbursts of anger, selfish rivalries, dissensions, factions, envying, murder, drunkenness, carousing, and similar things. "Therefore, the flesh in it corruptibility and all it filth, and sin will not and cannot stand in the presence of God.

Take this opportunity to pause for a minute and think of all the wrong things you have ever done. Also, think about all the wicked things that you can ever remember, heard, or seen that man has done. With all this put together, God still left all his glory and all the riches in heaven and came down to earth to die for your sins. When everything fails, God is the only one who will not fail you. His hands are ever ready to give you a hug, one that will wipe all your tears away and give you that peace of mind that can only come from God. This peace passes all understanding.

People will often wonder why you are always peaceful in the midst of all your problems and may want to know how you did it. Jesus died on the cross for you. He was wounded for your transgressions and was bruised for your iniquities. You are priceless in the sight of God. God can do anything for you. His love for you is unconditional and everlasting. It is not because of anything you did or what you did not do that made him to die for you, but because of the love, he has for you. God loved you while you were a sinner, and he knew you when you were nothing but a mess and a nobody, but he still loved and cared for you. The love of God, therefore cannot, be purchased. It is free and available for 'whosoever will.'

In fact, it is because of your situation that he came to die for you, so that you can trade all your sorrows, sins, and hopeless life for all his promises and for the joy of the Lord. God has promised us eternal life, good health, prosperity of all kind—you name it. If you are in bondage, God can set you free. Just ask him to come into your life, and he will. The Bible says that heaven rejoices over the salvation of one man. Any time I see a repentant sinner, my heart is full of joy and I imagine how the whole of the heavens will be rejoicing because of that one soul, which is gain for Jesus. You are simply loved by God.

I want to encourage you to take that big step in making this decision today. Think about it. A dead man cannot take all his inheritance on earth with him in the grave. No matter how hard you worked for your property, you will never take it with you when you die. What then would you have that is yours in death? What will it profit you to gain the whole world and lose your soul? Imagine a dying man struggling to save his life on earth only to die and rise up into an existence not expecting. After the entire struggle, he still dies to face another struggle; only this time it is everlasting. Any time I think about this, I cannot help but to praise the Lord for his saving grace and his love that surpasses all understanding.

The Devil will want to use words of condemnation just to kill your spirit and to bring you back to that place where you were hopeless and didn't know who you were, but now that you know who you are and how precious you are, don't spend your time arguing with the Devil. Speak the Word of God. Whose report will you believe: the testimony of the Devil or the testimony of God? Pay no attention to that one who tries to use words to destroy your faith and confidence in God. The Devil tries to ruin you and make you feel broken. It has been an old weapon of the Devil, which he is still using: words.

But, the scripture says we will overcome the Devil by the Word of God (the Scripture) and by the words of our testimonies.

Before you turn this page, I want you to ask yourself these questions. Am I born again? If I die today, can I make it to heaven? If you cannot answer yes to both questions, stop and think about it.

If you have never trusted in the Lord Jesus Christ as your Saviour, will you consider the prompting of the Holy Spirit as He speaks to your heart? You need to be born again. Will you pray the prayer of repentance and become a new creation in Christ today?

If you want to accept Jesus Christ as your Saviour and be born again; here is a simple prayer. Remember any other prayer will not save you. It is not one of those sophisticated prayer. This prayer is simply a way to express to God your faith in him and thank him for providing for your salvation. It is only trusting in Christ that can save you from sin. Believe in your heart that Jesus is Lord, confess with your mouth, and you shall be saved.

The Prayer of Repentance

God, I know that I have sinned against you and I deserve punishment. But, Jesus Christ took the punishment that I deserve so that through faith in Him I could be forgiven. I asked for your forgiveness. I believe you came down from heaven to die for my salvation and that you are God. Thank You for Your wonderful grace and forgiveness— the gift of eternal life Amen.

Have you made a decision to received Christ as your Lord and Saviour because of what you have read here? If so, please find a Bible-believing church to fellowship and they will help you to grow in your faith. I will also like to pray for you, so please contact me if you can. (Details printed in this book.) Remember the quickest way to grow is to read your Bible and pray every day. Please also send me any prayer request you may have. God bless you.

How I Became a Born-Again Christian

Being born again is a unique experience that can ever happen in any one's life. For me, it's life changing and couldn't have been better. It's a decision that I made by faith, having been convinced and satisfied of his unfailing and unconditional love to all mankind and the quality of life to them who believe in Him.

It has also been my desire to tell the world of my experience of being born again. I cannot say when exactly I became a born-again Christian. But, it was some time in 1993. It was kind of a process for me.

From the time I read and heard about Jesus, I sought to find out who is this Jesus and why do people who call themselves 'born-again Christians' possess powers, such as the power to forgive, deliverance to heal and be healed, give, and love beyond our human understanding. During the time I was seeking the presence of the Lord Jesus, I became saved.

In 1993, I picked up a magazine called *'Soon'*, which I found on the ground and began to read. I was amazed at the testimonies of the people I read in the magazine. I can remember one said he/ she had healed from the deadly HIV AIDS disease in the name of Jesus! It was amazing. At the end of all these testimonies there was something about being born again that intrigued me. I began to question myself and started thinking deeply about this Jesus mentioned in the magazine; and what is 'born again.' *How can one be born again? Why should one be born again? Who is this Jesus? What is so different and important about him and the people who believed in him?*

My Background

I was born into a religious Christian family. We went to church every Sunday and tried to do good works, but I never knew who this Jesus is. In my urge to find an answer to the question, my younger sister Elizabeth came home one day and announced that a friend of hers invited her to Scripture Union and she was now a born-again Christian. I can recalled how we laughed at her. The Devil made it sound like some kind of a cult to us. Even though I had read about this in the magazine and was looking for answers, I just could not suddenly relate or identify it right in my home.

My sister suddenly became different. No amount of provocation could hurt her, and in fact, she became more loving, caring, and prayerful. I watched her closely and was honestly impressed of the changes in her behaviours and attitudes towards everything else that she did. I actually love the new person. One day, I decided to listen to her preaching and she invited me to the Scripture Union. At the Scripture Union, I began to understand in a broader and deepening meaning of the love of Christ and my sinful deeds which included my wrongly behaviours towards my sister amount to ignorant sin, and for once found answers to some of my question. I was deeply touched by; the genuine love and energy that came from these people I meet at the Scripture Union. They were happy people who loved their God and, interestingly, most of them were my age and ordinary people like me.

I wanted to be part of that experience, so I began to read my Bible. At about the same time, people I came across seemed to want to tell me about Jesus. The Bible became so alive to me, I began to see and understand the spiritual things of God. I was happier than I was when I joined that congregation, this decision and the motoring helped me with self-control over peer pressure.

I became fearless of demonic powers and felt more secure and confident in my Jesus. With prayers and continual fellowship, I came to understand further Jesus ministries, and soon I had this power to love every man and the urge to tell them about the Jesus that I had found. I developed a personal relationship with Jesus, and in that same year (1993), I decided to accept or make a full declaration about letting the Lord become my personal Saviour and Lord over all things including my decisions by praying fervently before taking any decision.

Thereafter, I became born again! This is how I became a disciplined follower of Jesus and a true Christian. Before I became born again, I was very shy. I only talked when I was with people known to me personally. However, when I gave my life to Jesus, I became bold and could speak in public. I preached the gospel in public places and could approach anyone to tell them about the good news of Jesus. My self-esteem improved extraordinarily.

Amazingly, whenever I see someone, the love of God in me causes me to want to tell them about Jesus, and I have the urgency to tell them about Jesus so they too can be saved and make it to heaven. I also did it to please God. I knew if I won a soul for Jesus, he was going to be very pleased with me, so I preached to all my friends at schools and Colleagues, the marketplace and people I met on the way. I will purposely board the public bus to preach the gospel of Jesus and just anyone I came across. I was full with overflowing love of God and went about looking for people I could give some of this newfound love in my life.

I was also, privileged to have attended the Freetown Bible Training Centre, where I learnt the Word of God. With enthusiasm and revelation, I received the gospel of Jesus and the understanding of the Scriptures. Eventfully, God directed me to the Scripture Union (SU) where, by election and prayer, I was call to be in the youth leadership committee (central meeting). Central meeting is where young people, mostly teenagers, of all secondary schools in Freetown meet every Friday. There I was also, trained to be a God-fearing leader with the Word of God. I also had the opportunity to have positively influence over others and to win souls for Jesus.

Let me take this opportunity to encourage you to find such Bible-believing centre as a young Christian to get involved, as this will serve profitable for your Christian growth. Perhaps the best decision you might take in your lifetime. One thing you must know is Christianity without the Holy Spirit is worthless.

I hope that as you read this encounter, you will find Jesus in your own unique way. I pray that you find a spiritual rebirth that will change your life forever. I love you with the love of the Lord. Amen.

Chapter 2

What Is Your Purpose on Earth?

I believe this is a question everyone should ask him or herself. I became born again at the age of about seventeen going on eighteen years old. Most of my youthful days, were indeed dedicated to preaching and engaging in the things of God. I felt fulfilled and satisfied doing the things of God such as: studying his Word, fellowshipping with other Christian, praying, evangelising, and working in the faith.

It was perfect. Being active in church is, however, not sufficient to confirm that you are working in God's will. Although it is a right thing to do as it helps your Christian life to grow and it also encourages others; at times, we can get so caught up in performing our duties in church that we can at times miss the will of God for our life if.

As Christians, we are the body of Christ, and we all have a part to play in the body of Christ. It may be the cause that, we are supposed to operate as an arm in the body of Christ yet we are busy operating as a leg. By doing so, you will not experience the full potential of Christ in your life.

In some cases, one will merely be playing church and or religion. It becomes a routine rather than a relationship or daily walk with Christ. Our Christian work with God is all about Him and not about us; God requires a selfless attitude in our calling as a Christian. We must allow Jesus to teach us how to operate in his body. Walking in your own understanding and strength will eventually bring you to failure and weariness.

Growing Up

In my life experience as a young woman, I was faced with the trauma and being a victim of a civil war in Sierra Leone. I experienced an unexpected change in my life. I was born into a respectable, religious, loving, and caring family. My parents were very responsible towards us as children, and I grew up seeing my parents working very hard to give us the best.

Until the outbreak of the war in Sierra Leone, I had never experienced hardship or in my entire life thought, of been forced to flee from my home unexpectedly. I faced with the trauma of being a victim of war (like most Sierra Leoneans). I experienced an unexpected change in my life that needed a drastic decision made, one that shifted my life into a new destination.

I was full with shock, hatred, and bitterness of this event. I thought *who gave these rebels the right to steal my life.* I thought I was been robbed from my sweet family home, my education, good friends, a brighter future, and so on. Nevertheless, I thank God for Jesus, who is the supplier of our needs and who causes all things to work together for good to them that love the Lord. My flight to Gambia, I must say, was not an easy journey in that boat lost in the sea. I experienced the supernatural of God, and by faith in Jesus, I landed in the beautiful land of Gambia.

Having fled to Gambia with my mother, two sisters, and little brother to save our life, I became a complete stranger in a foreign land—very inexperience and no clue of how I should continue with my life. Though confused, I had hope in Jesus. Hope that he is able to take care of my family and me and to complete what he had started in me.

My determination was to acquire those things that been taken from me. I worked very hard in Gambia, landing a role as a volunteer for charity work and all the time working closely with a local church in Gambia. Eventually, God directed me to further my studies in the United Kingdom. At the time, it was the best thing that could have ever happened to me. It was a dream come true!

I tried to find ways to success and said to myself, 'I will never let these rebels win.' I had the determination to achieve those things I been robbed from. I got so angry that I had drawn away by the desire to be successful and to make some achievement in my life. Thinking this alone will help by situation.

My active work with Jesus in Gambia involved engaged work as a volunteer for charities and played an important role in my local church in Gambia. As the youth president of a local church, I engaged young people with the Word of God and tried to develop their Christian relationship with God to the best of God's ability in me.

I really had some blessed memories in Gambia. To finish, I was favoured and got a visa to study in the United Kingdom. I thought this was the best thing that could ever happen to me, it was a dream come through. I had dream of furthering my studies in England for as long as I could remember. I always dreamt of living the English life as shown in the television. As an English literature student, I had loved English writers, drama and poets and I had imaginations or perceptions of how life in England would be: beautiful, colourful trees in spring; white winter; romantic showers of rain; the experience of using the underground . . . I could go on forever.

Coming to England: The English Dream

When I arrived in the United Kingdom in 1999, I was extremely happy. It compensated for the trauma I had gone through, caused by

23

the civil war in my country, and I was comforted. At least I could get that England experience I desired from youth: to study and experience life in the United Kingdom.

However, I was also disappointed that I could not find a reviving Bible-believing church to attend. My perception was that Christianity came from England, therefore finding a church would not be a problem. I thought that the majority of the people in England were practising Christians and that everyone went to church on Sunday. This was in addition to thinking about meeting with all those great men of God I had read about or seen in television. I was honestly shocked at the church-going Christian culture of the British people.

At first, I did not have any Christian friends who can encourage me in the things of God. I remembered the first time I tried to evangelize to a classmate and I felt like some alien. I had never met anyone who boldly and proudly denounces God, and I was sincerely shocked. In Sierra Leone, we are multicultural and people practise different religions, but it is very unlikely to find someone who openly and proudly says there is no God or say he/she does not practise any religion. This was a culture shock to me. (God bless)

By then, I found life in the United Kingdom extremely difficult. The climate was different, and I could not understand the system. One has to pay tax for any utility used. Formerly, in my country, you use water freely and no tax are been levied on housing. Most people own their land, houses, and we all watch TV freely. Most of all, as a student, I had immigration restrictions. I just did not know where to start life in the United Kingdom. I was a displaced young woman who landed in a foreign land faced with immigration-control laws.

It is not uncommon, to find someone confronted with desperate situations in his or her life. For instance, the Bible tells us in the New Testament that Jesus and his family fled to Egypt after an angel of the Lord had appeared to Joseph in a dream and had warned him of the plan of King Herod to kill Jesus. Jesus's family had to relocate for fear of losing their life. From that Scripture, we can see that Jesus knew what it meant to be a foreigner under immigration control. He lived in a foreign land until the death of King Herod, and from that, I knew that Jesus understood my plight and knew my fears. Esther was a young girl who lived in a foreign land yet had the favour of a king. What am I saying? I learnt that it does not matter what your problems might be, whether you experience a change of location, where you are, where you came from, or where you are going. Only one God reigns in majesty over all creations.

Scripture tells us that the government of this world is upon the shoulder of God. God, therefore, has control over all the functioning in this world, and he is the same yesterday, today, and forever. This God is able to turn your mourning into gladness and has the power to put everything in place for your good. He understands and is able to take care of you. However, this does not mean you will evade life's little problems. It means God will make you an overcomer as you accept Jesus as your Lord and Saviour. You will overcome every time you call upon him.

Working without the Anointing

Scripture says, 'unless the Lord builds the house they labour in vain that build it: unless the Lord keeps the city, the watchman, wakes, but in vain' (Psalm 127:1).

From this, we see that for anyone's dreams, aspirations, and ambitions to translate into a sustainable outcome, you must seek or consult with the Lord for his anointing to come upon it. To simplify, the anointing of God is the active power of the Holy Spirit working in us and through us as present in you. Christianity without the Holy Spirit is dead. Having the hands of God in everything about you and making God the paramount control of your visions as the dream giver and making him increase and magnify him in your business will earn you affluence in a unique way. Because God's increase is your physical prosperity and spiritual wisdom, this is what you find in the manifestation in the physical realm.

If you are reading this book, and you have been walking in your own understanding without allowing the anointed one of God—who is Christ Jesus, to take control of your life entirely. It is my prayer for you that God will, by his infinite mercy and redeeming quality, deliver you from the forces of darkness and all the strategies of the Devil to lead you into failure.

May the good God Almighty give to your insight the revelation of the power and presence of God's Holy Spirit available through Jesus Christ to you as a believer of Christ, in Jesus's name, I have prayed. Amen.

My Battles

I struggled to compile both work and school at the same time. As I fought to be successful, I found myself drawing away from God so slowly that I even did not realise that my Christian life was not the same as it used to be. I was not reading my Bible again, nor did I have the time to pray as I used to. In addition, the things that did not worry me before were those that I found myself worrying. Although I am naturally a quiet-natured person, I also noticed that I was struggling with being shy, this was something that I was totally, I should say, 'delivered from.' From my experience as a Christian, I know when needing wakeup call and draw closer to Jesus.

When we are working, in Christ, we received boldness, we can do all things through Christ who strengthen us, but outside Christ, we are just as ordinary like everyone else. We become a powerless Christian and very feeble to the devil. A religious action or self-delusion about the state of one's relationship with God does not mean you are what you think. In another word by just thinking, you are holy or righteous does not make you holy or righteous.

Likewise, I was not a bad person in my eyes. I did not see or accepted the fact that I had drawn from God. I tried and lived life as a good person, but without the help of the Holy Spirit.

I realized that no matter how I tried and how much I achieved, I was still not happy. Anytime I succeeded in doing one thing, I desired another, and so it was as though I never really succeeded at all.

The economists say humans' needs are unlimited, but the means of meeting those need are limited. I am here to tell you that 'the means' to meeting all of our needs can only be found in Jesus. 'But my God shall supply all your need, according to his riches in glory, by Christ Jesus' (Philippians 4:19). Since I had realised my previous effortless actions without the blessings of God, and make do my homework to correct my mistake and involved Jesus in my plans and objective, I have become happier in all my achievements. I am happy with the family I have, my educational gains, and spiritual growth and more. I no longer feel helpless in wanting self-development. I am simple happy.

When I walked outside God's will, I had a constant gap in my life, which I could not fill or satisfy. Nothing seemed to have worked for me, and I became the number one worrier in the world. My life was so empty and I felt lost. There was a gap in my life and I needed it to be filled and free. Confused and dismayed, I became hot tempered, and just one word from anyone could set me ablaze. To make matter worse, thought I had a good job at the time I did not like it. I felt like a prisoner on the job. This was because I was working because of the financial gain the job gave me and not because it was something, I enjoy doing. Although the job was very flexible with my then schedule, and the pay was more competitive than the company's competitors were, there was always this pressure of something that I could not just understand.

As I pondered and sought ways to find answers to my questions, the Lord came to my rescue. I remembered the blessed day the Holy Spirit came upon me like a peaceful dove with an outpouring of love. I had not felt this way for years. Having examined my life and in that state of mind, I asked myself, 'What is the purpose of my life? Why was I born into this earth?' I searched my life with all the qualification I had gained, all the things I so desired, and it did not mean anything to me at that moment. I thought what it should profit me if I am to gain the whole world and lose my soul. This thought open my eyes to see what is around me. I gave myself a reality check in line with the scriptures. Our mind and thinking is a powerful tool to a successful walk with God. If you can grasp the power of the resurrection of Jesus Christ and know who you are in him then you have found the answer to peaceful life now and eternal life.

With this, I then realised how far I had gone from God but also recognized that all these years I could have been dead and gone and could not have made it to heaven. But, God had been so gracious to me and Jesus had been interceding on my behalf. Glory be to God, he saved me. He gave me a second chance.

I began to count my blessings and name them one by one. I then also realised that God had been faithful to me. Overwhelmed by his unfailing love, such impeccable peace I received from God, and on that August day, I wept, as I had never done before. At the end, I made a decision to make God the master of my life. I cut off working on a Sunday and decided to give that day to the Lord. I began going to church on Sunday to fellowship and take time to praise and thank God for his goodness towards me. In addition, to commit in rebuilding my Christian life and relationship with God and others, as I drew closer to God he also drew closer to me. He drew closer to me than I did.

It was a very hard decision for me to make, as my Sunday wage was time and a half, and I only worked part time. This was my sacrifice as a way to say thank-you to God. God's perfect love moved me to take such a decision and I have never regretted it.

Gradually, as I began to read the Bible and pray, I became more peaceful. Nothing seemed to worry me anymore, and I was happy. My life began to change and people that are around me began to ask questions. They thought something was different about me, but they just could not figure out what was different.

As I got closer to God, God began to open my eyes, and by revelation, God began to show me his will for my life. God transformed my thoughts and heart. He began to teach me spiritual things, and my eyes opened and I saw that the plans of God for my life are for good and not for evil. They are plans for me to prosper and for me to have good health and not to die. God perfected his love in me and this is why I want to reach out to everyone I could through this book, so if you are going through one problem or the other as a Christian you will have hope in Jesus and his saving grace as he delivers you. I believe anyone can experience such quality of life and for you to know the purpose of your life.

Breaking Free

The purpose of your life surpasses all your needs and personal fulfilment, and all those things that you so desire to achieve that you think will make you happy. These needs are such as to belong in a relationship, society or to have shelter, family, career, wealth, power, and all your ambitions. Remember, as mentioned earlier, God is able to take care of all your needs. He knows your requisites for life. However, the purpose of your life has nothing to do with all of those things of the flesh. When we are catch up with the worries of life people tend to want to do anything to fulfil their desires. They covet, lie, cheat, slander and do all sort of things. Some engaged in witchcraft and all manner of evil and satanic work of the devil.

Jesus came to set us free from the bondage of toiling to fulfil our satisfaction and desire. He came to give us life. He came to set us free from the fear of death. Nevertheless, how many of God's people, know this today. Christian people are finding with the same problems as non-Christians and they look for answers to their problems the same way a non-Christian will do. The God purpose of your life is to add super to the natural giving you a supernatural life.

If we are ignorant of the complete work of Jesus Christ, the accomplished work of Jesus when Jesus died on the cross then it is very unlikely for us to know God plans and purpose for us. By dyeing on the cross Jesus did not only brought us eternal salvation but also freedom and totality of wholeness. We need to gain spiritual knowledge to experience this freedom.

We had learnt that we are, created by God and he did so for a purpose. This is a revelation that the Devil will not want you to know. The purpose of God for your life does not subject to the circumstances that surround you. Your abilities or disabilities, age or location, cannot control the will of God for your life. How can we possibly know the purpose of God in our life?

Discovering Your Purpose on Earth
By Knowing Your Creator

The first step to you knowing your purpose on earth is to realise that you are God's creation, and the only way you will get an answer as to why you were born is from your creator. I have had people ask—why God brought them into this world only to make them suffer. But my question is this: why did God choose you to be born into this world and not the many eggs your mother carried? What is the uniqueness of your God-given egg? Can you really be the captain of your own ship?

Now let us look in to the Scriptures and see if we can find some answers to our questions.

The Bible tells us in the book of Genesis that, the spirit of God lives in all humankind; we created by God and for his purpose. We have the spirit of God in us; until we put God in the rightful place in our life, our life remains incomplete. God created man and placed a gap in man's heart that can only filled by God.

We see people searching to find answers to their lives; in order to fill that gap; they have taken so many paths. They are confused and do not know where to start or what to do. Some people go the extra miles by travelling to other places seeking to find that ultimate fulfilment of their spirit. They start by realising that there is something more to their ordinary life and seek to find answers by themselves. They seek to determine what they want to be or identify their dreams and how they can achieve set goals and ambitions in their lives. They anticipate. By so doing, they will determine their purpose of life and fill the empty gap in their life. It will never work that way. God created man and placed a gap in man's heart and he alone can fill it. And no one in Christianity can ever be the captain of his or her own ship.

Until you call on God and ask him to come into your life, you will remain unfulfilled. We have heard about stories of rich people testifying that their riches did not give them true happiness, and poverty will certainly not qualify for that.

You were made by God and for God and life is about following with your maker and letting Him use you for his purposes. This purpose we can only know through our God and maker. We could try our best, but we do not have the full capacity to have ultimate control over our life. This is why you and I do not know the exact time or place when we will die.

God made man out of love and so that we can fellowship with Him and be His friend. The Bible tells us in Genesis that God came down in the cool of the day to look for Adam. I can imagine God talking and reasoning with Adam, making plans together with Adam. Saying words like, 'Adam, what do you think about the colour of this flower?' and Adam says, 'Only you, Lord, can work in such perfection.' in Genesis, God gave the responsibility of naming all the animal and birds on earth to Adam. God called Abraham his friend because they had a relationship. This is one of the purposes of God for man—to have a relationship and followership with him. Drawing our self from God brings separation that will affect our spirit man.

There is a spiritual bond between God and man; God created a place in man's heart that cannot be filled by anything else but God himself. We learn that God loved man and wanted to share all his creation with man. The psalmist says, what is man that God is so mindful of him and made him a little lower than himself. God is mindful of us, meaning He genuinely care for us. God knows the purpose of your life. He knows the role he wants you to play in his creation.

It is our part to seek God and to discover his purpose on earth for our life. However, you cannot do that by yourself, which is why God sends us the Holy Spirit who will show and direct us in discovering our purpose on earth. No one is an identity mistake. Our true identity and purpose for life is in God through Jesus Christ, our Lord and Saviour.

The way in which you can discover the purpose of God in your life is by going back to the creator. You must have to communicate with him. Imagine yourself being a qualified and professional pilot with many years of experience. Due to technological advancement, new aircraft introduced that fits and meets the twenty-first-century challenge. Of course, being a pilot, and no matter your experience and qualifications, may never guarantee your ability to understand the new system and fly the new aircraft without the manufacturer's demo software or owner's manual detailing the various operating systems, gargets, and electronic buttons.

The only way you can be able to know the use of it and its operations is to read the owner's manual of that aircraft. The inventor will enclose a manual for the aircraft, which will tell the pilot the purpose of the aircraft and how it can work. Likewise, accepting Jesus as your Lord and Saviour, or being born again, is the first step to take in knowing your creator. When you give your life to the Lord, you are in the position to establish a relationship with him, and with time, you will grow in this relationship. God will reveal and show you his will and purpose for you through the Holy Spirit. The Bible states that true worshipers will worship in spirit and the just will live by faith.

The Bible tells us that Jesus is always close to us; we just need to open up to him (Revelation 3:20). God loves us, and according to John 17:3, God's plan is that we might know him. So to know the purpose of God, you will have to refer to the manual of God, which is the Bible, the Word of God.

Knowing God your maker gives you confidence in your faith as a Christian; it empowers you and develops your faith. God wants us to seek him, he said, when we seek him, we will find him. He will reveal Himself to us so we can know Him. Knowing how big or powerful or loving your God is, put you in the position of confidence. Jesus is the way and the truth. The way to everlasting life and truth is his word. You will know the truth, and the truth will set you free.

Through the Word of God

The words of God tell us how to recognise ourselves. They teach us the purpose for our being (Acts 17:28).

As pointed out earlier, there is opportunity granted to us to make individually led decisions. This is predominantly the radioactive period in everyone's life. The instability in hearts and minds of any individual is potentially the very dangerous times to resist putting God's words before us and to confirm God's words by faith.

Aligning your heart and mind with God's Word should constitute the positioning of oneself with Christ Jesus, because, this is the only way we can get to God and the beginning of seeking the knowledge of God. For Jesus is the way, the truth, and the life.

The Bible tells us that no one can go to the father except through Jesus; you must have a relationship with Jesus Christ. You must be born again and become part of the body of Christ. A way to continue and to build your new Christian life is to read your Bible. In reading your Bible, your faith in God increases. Your mind will be, transformed. You will no longer think carnally but you will have the mind-set of the Spirit of God (John 3:15).

As born-again Christians, God gave us the power and the ability to think right and to make good and positive decision by ourselves. This anointing is upon all Christians who are born again and not just on selected few. I had seen Christians born again but totally dependent upon their pastors. They cannot do or take any decision in life by themselves without consulting their pastors. Some, I believe, is because of lack of their personal devotional life with the Word of God.

I see in the church, people do not want the responsibility that comes with this personal freedom. They chose to remain dependent upon someone else. They would rather take a shortcut rather than read the Scriptures and pray to God by themselves. Others, perhaps, do so because they believe their pastor's decision is the right one and they are not capable in making such decision by themselves. We thank God for our pastors, whom God has given the special gift and calling to minister in the house of God. However, I want to encourage you not to be one of those who contribute aimlessly to overwhelm our pastors with problems that can best solved by our Lord Himself.

Those who are committed with great fear not to make decisions without first consulting their pastors, and not God, might think they do not have the anointing to take divine decisions and that their pastors do. These sorts of perception misrepresent the Word of God. You do not need permission from others to think or apply God's Word in life. This is not, however, a passport to disobey your leaders in church. Remember there is order in the house of the Lord. As Christian, we give honour to who honour is due.

The calling of a pastor is recognise by God and is subject to God's authority. Pastor are usually anointed man or woman of God but not one that is to be worship by anyone or take the freedom God has freely given to us.

As a believer, you can speak the Word of God and things will happen. You and your pastors have the same gift: the gift of salvation by Christ Jesus. Accordingly, John 3:16 said, 'For God so love the world that he gave his only begotten son that whosoever believe should not perish but have everlasting life.' When Jesus died on the cross, he died to set us free from slavery and dependence; and whom the Son set free is free indeed. The Bible says let the weak say I am strong and let the poor say I am rich.

When you repented from your sin and gave your life to Jesus as your Lord and Saviour, something spiritually happens: you received power. You became a renew person and received power over satanic attack, power over sickness, poverty, oppression, and the sort. You cannot know these things if you do not spend time with the Word of God. Please, see Acts 17:11. You need to take time to read the Bible so you can know by yourself your position in Christ Jesus, so your mind-set will be renewed and attuned to the Word of God.

It is at this point when our mind-set renewed with the Word of God, we are victorious in life. At that point, all things are possible by faith in God's Word through Christ Jesus, our Saviour. God expects us to behave like kingdom children because that's what we are made of when we became born again.

I want to encourage you to renew your mind on a daily basis. Meditate on the Word of God. Bring your mind-set to the Word of God. The salvation of Christ brought us deliverance. You can think, talk, walk, and do all things like Jesus. The responsibility of the pastor is to pray with us and intercede for us but never to make the decision for us as the question of who makes the decision, whether about our future relationships, jobs, marriages, education, or health, including the decision about business adventures; these rests upon us.

This last resort is the ultimate freedom we are, accorded by the spirit of God and by the sacrifices made by our Lord Jesus Christ to the effect that those who believe are immediately set free. And young Christians are spiritually aided to full freedom as they abide in the Word of our Lord Jesus (John 8:31-36).

Who Controls Your Mind?

The reason why you bring your mind-set to the Word of God is who has control over your mind-set controls you. That is why God places the salvation of Jesus over our head as a helmet so that the Devil will not have power over us ever again.

It is also, meant for our protection—protection for our head, which is our mind-set. 'And take the helmet of salvation, and the sword of the Spirit, which is the Word of God' (Ephesians 6:17). Our salvation assured and seal by the blood of Jesus, and our protection from every evil attracts from the Devil the adversary is in Jesus. The Word of God has life and they are living.

By reading the Word of God, you will learn so many secrets of life that will lead you to success. This is why we see God admonish Joshua in Joshua 1:8. He says, 'Do not let this book of the law departs from you, but thou shall meditate upon it day and night.' The Word of God also tells us in 1 Corinthians 12 that there are different parts in the body of Christ, just as any other body, and each part of the body has its function/gifts.

All the parts of the body work together as one body. The bible says that to some God gives the gifts of tongues and faith while to others the gifts of prophecy and interpreting tongues. So unless you became a part of God's body, you will not be able to identify which part of God's body you are or belong to, nor will you identify your gifts/functioning that you possess.

The Bible tells us that the Word of God is never lies, which means everything that you can read in the Bible is the truth and certain.

You can never go wrong with the Bible. In Hebrews 12, the Bible tells us that the Word of God is sharper than any two-edged sword. It is life and living, active, going about doing what it was ask to do—just as it did in the beginning when God created the world. The Bible tells us that in the beginning, God said, 'Let there be light and there was light' so when we speak the Word of God as it is in the Bible, the Bible tells us that it will never go forth and come back to us without accomplishing what it was purposed for. It will do that which it sent to do. For example, when the Word of God says, 'No weapon forged against you will prevail, and you will refute every tongue that accuses you,' this is exactly what it means. Amen. When the Word of God spoken in season according to your situation, it does what it says or means.

The world contradicts everything the Word of God stands for. This means if you are to seek answers in the Word of God, you must totally believe in the Scripture as spoken by God. Peter believed and walked on water. Elijah called down fire from heaven. Barren Hannah became the mother of a great prophet name Samuel. When applying the Word of God, which is the Scriptures as found in the Bible, in your life, you might look stupid and might not make sense to others, but if you believe by faith, you will see the result.

Taking one-step of faith after the other is like taking steps towards a bright light afar. The more steps you take forward, the clearer the sight, and when you eventually get closer, you see clearly; you emerge in the light. At that point, you see everything is possible with God. This is why the Bible tells us that it is impossible to please God without faith.

It is humanly impossible for any man to walk on water, but Peter did. I'm sure when Peter called to Jesus and said he was going to meet Jesus by walking on the water, the other disciples of Jesus would have said many things in their head. Such as, *not again, big mouth Peter, Show-off. You must be joking*. By faith, he walked on water. In the kingdom of God, by faith in God impossibilities are possible.

By Prayer

You can also discover your purpose on earth through prayers. We communicate to God through prayers. Ephesians 6:18 tells us that we must never stop praying. Prayer is the fastest way to communicate to God. We speak to God when we pray and God speaks back to us in our answered prayers. Prayer can increase your intimacy with God through Christ. Through prayer, God can reveal the supernatural things of the world to you or, to be precise, you will encounter miracles in your particular situation.

There are different types of prayers in the Bible, but the one I will emphasize is the prayer that will lead us to a devotional righteousness and a personal relationship with Jesus, the one Jesus talked about in Matthew 6:6. Jesus talked about having private time with the Lord.

You and God only hear this private prayer. A private prayer is the type of prayer that you can only say to God. This type of prayer brings intimacy with God. It causes you to draw closer to God, and as you see your prayers answered, you know that it is the work of God in your life.

This devotional prayer life will open your eyes to experience supernatural things on earth and know beyond doubt that you can do all things through Christ who strengthen you (Philippians 4:13).

Prayer is a way of seeking and communicating with God. I personally see it as God is in a secret place but wants us to find him. He said, when we seek Him, we will find Him. A way to seek God is through prayer. Through prayer, God will reveal himself to you and you will find your answers to life. Your purpose on earth will made known to you and you will find ways in walking in your purpose.

God can speak to you in many ways: through the Holy Spirit, his Word, through others or angels, and in some cases, directly to us like in the case of Samuel. (Read 1 Samuel.)

In discovering the purpose of God in your life, you will come to know how precious you are in the sight of God. The Bible tells us in Zachariah 2:8, 'For this is what the Lord Almighty says: "After he has honoured me and has sent me against the nations that have plundered you—for whoever touches you touches the apple of his eye."'

For those with an identity dilemma, I want to tell you that Jesus loves you dearly and he died for you on the cross. You are as equally important to God as the rest of the world, but you need to get to the Word of God by yourself to find the answers to your questions. You will also discover that you were not a mistake. God speaks to everyone differently and in the language, we understand.

God created everyone for a purpose. Your parents may not have planned to have you, but God did. You have every reason to appreciate and love yourself. The Bible tells us in Psalm 139:14 that the psalmist praises God for his appearances. 'I will praise thee, for I am fearfully and wonderfully made: marvellous are thy works; and that my soul knoweth right well.' God actually took his time in making you, in that you are fearfully and wonderfully made in the image and likeness of God.

Your schoolteacher might have thought you were less than average or amounted to no good, but God says, You can do all things through Christ who gives you strength (Philippians 4:13). God uses the very foolish things and remnants of man to perform His miracle and make the wise and able useless, so that only He can take the glory.

We must learn to appreciate and like ourselves. A person is born a woman or a man for a purpose. It is not by chance or by accident, or even luck or fate, that we were born. We were born as we are because God wanted us to be born that way. The part of the world you were born in, the colour of your skin, or the family you were born into does not matter to God. The salvation of God is not subject to any of these things but made available to whosoever will.

When I tell people about Jesus I do not care of things like the colour of the skin or the cloth one were, look, status or any of the sort but I give the person the gospel of Jesus. I encourage people to take the gospel just as they are. The rest is up to Jesus.

Take a minute to think about it. Biologically, a woman carries millions of eggs in her womb. Why not the other eggs your mother is still carrying or carried regardless, God chose you. It is because he has a purpose for your life. He wanted someone with your kind of mouth, nose, character, and attitude, with a lifespan like yours to perform a certain task in the world at a particular period.

Yes, one may be an illegitimate child according to the law of the land, but that does not determine one's destiny. By accepting Jesus as your Lord and Saviour, you became a legitimate child of the kingdom of the most high. How you walk with Jesus and your understanding of your new birth will change your perception for life.

God made us all and he knows us more than we know ourselves. The Bible tells us in Matthew 10:30 that God even knows the number of hairs on our head. I have yet to meet anyone who can tell me the number of hairs on their head. This confirms that God knows us more than we know ourselves.

Peter was a man whom we all know was quick to talk; he was hot tempted. Peter was ready to fight to save the life of Jesus. However, when Jesus asked, 'Who do men say I am?' it was Peter that God gave the revelation: 'Say thou are the son of God.' Paul was a rich and learned man, a man perfect in the matter of law and religious observation. Timothy was a timid boy. Nevertheless, that does not stop God from using them.

Naomi was a widow and Esther was a slave girl. Rachael was a prostitute. Thomas doubted. There are all kinds of characters in the Bible. God has a purpose for you. You can start by accepting him as your Lord and Saviour, then you will be saved and discover the purpose of God in your life.

Salvation is open to all as long as you welcome him into your heart. We saw Saul, who was very zealous in killing Christians, had an encounter with Jesus on his way to his mission to kill Christians. In that encounter, God changed him. Saul became Paul, who later preached the gospel of Jesus throughout his lifetime.

God has a purpose for you. He knitted you in your mother's womb. Again you can start by accepting him as your Lord and Saviour, and then you will be saved and discover the purpose of God in your life. It is only a man's spirit that knows the thought of a man so is the Spirit of God. Your Spirit is what keeps your body alive, it is the real you. We die when our spirt leaves our body. Therefore, both the Spirit and the body works together in unity to keeps us a life When you accept Jesus as your Lord and Saviour, the Spirit of God will come into your life and reveal the heart of God to you.

Please, I beseech to respond to the promptness of the Holy Spirit and make Jesus your Lord and Saviour and be born again. If you are already born again, why not make today (if you have not done so) the day when you make that decision to renew your calling as a Christian and your strength in Jesus, the day when you acceptably surrender your all to him? Jesus is waiting for you to ask Him to come into your life. I encourage you to take that bold steps today!

Chapter 3

Be Prepared for Trials and Temptations

It is very easy to assume that being a born-again Christian is a life free from all earthly problems, especially when you are new to the walk with Christ. People often think it is a life full of roses or like sleeping in a bed of roses. What we sometimes fail to realise is that, though we are born again, we are still man on earth. We are presently, faced with all the laws that govern and rule the earth.

The good news is the Bible tells us in 2 Peter 2:9, 'If this is so, then the Lord knows how to rescue godly men from trials and to hold the unrighteous for the Day of Judgment, while continuing their punishment.' I want to encourage you never to give up in Christ. For every trial and temptation you face, there is an abundance of God's grace to overcome it buttressed with blessings or rewards at the end.

Lot was a righteous man, the nephew of Abraham, and he lived in Sodom and Gomorrah. Lot was rescued by God's angels while God totally destroy the city and its ungodly people. God did not destroy Lot and his household in Sodom and Gomorrah because of God's faithfulness to his servant, Abraham. God is always faithful to his word. As born-again Christians, Jesus overcame the Devil for our sake and has promised us a victorious life. Just as Lot was rescued, so we too will be rescued by God from the wickedness of this world. The righteous will not suffer for the wicked.

The Bible tells us in the first chapter of the book of James that Christians are to consider it pure joy when faced with all kinds of trials and temptations. But you may want to know why. Why should a Christian go through trials and temptation in the first place? The question to the answer still lies within the same chapter of James. The reason, according to James 1, is it's in trials and temptations that the testing of our faith develops and becomes stronger through perseverance. Our trails and temptations actually lead to our personal development and growth in our Christian life. They give us maturity and perfect our love for Christ.

Trials and temptations can be a sign of testing of our faith. It is by the testing of our faith we develop perseverance. Now let us assume that perseverance is in the form of a straight line. To persevere halfway from the beginning of the line does not qualify you for completion. You must go all the way to the very end. If we look carefully in the book of James, we see that the Bible does not say if we endure *some* or *certain types* of trials or temptations that this qualifies us for completion, not lacking any thing. It says 'all.' Every part. Every single aspect of each and every type of trial and temptation, the entire scenario of the matter.

I am familiar with people believing God for something in their life. They came to God and prayed while expecting an instant reply. They are zealous for a while, but as the days add to weeks and weeks to months, and sometimes months to years, they give up on God.

There are times when God answers our prayers promptly, according to the situation. At another time, he may wait for the right time, which might take a little longer than we anticipate. But we must trust God and have faith that He is able to answer our prayers.

In order for you to be complete, you must endure in faith until something happens. You may be thinking, *how will I know that something good will happen?* This is the very beginning of the testing of your faith. Believing in the Word of God that what you are hoping for will happen, even though you have not seen the result.

Remember according to the Bible in Hebrew 11:1 that faith is being sure of what we hope for and are certain of what we do not see.

For example, you hope to get married or that one day your drug-addicted child set free from such addiction. You hope for healing of any kind of sickness or disease, and even though it has not happened at the time you hoped for, you believed, you are sure beyond doubt that, because the Word of God says it is possible, you believed, it has happen and well with you. The Bible tells us that it is this type of faith, which is accounted to us as righteousness. Believing and totally trusting in God according to his Word. To exercise such a strong faith is to lock God's Word in action. As Psalm 119 put it, 'Forever, o Lord, Your word is settled in heaven' (Psalm 119:89). It bears no limitation to itself and is not limited by deeds but by the spirit in accordance with God's planning, says the Lord.

In your trials and temptations, you hope that God will help you. In hoping, your faith begins to work; perseverance kicks in and builds your faith. This faith is then accounted to you as righteousness.

Now many blessings are destined for a person who has faith. Righteousness is just a fragment of what you will enjoy when you apply the wisdom of faith in God in all your trials and temptations. You will be sure to have joy at the end.

The greatest faith of salvation through Jesus Christ is what I will like to encourage you to have in this book of *The Transformation Believer.* The person of Jesus Christ did not bring to us religion, nor did he bring condemnation to this sinful world, but he brought salvation to humanity. Christ loved the sinner; He accepted all who came to Him and freely gave the gift of life. Jesus healed the sick and set the captive free. The Bible tells us that he cared and healed all the sick and touched every life that came to him when he walked on earth. If you can dear to believe and have faith in the Scriptures to accept this Jesus as your Lord and Saviour, your life will never be the same. Only accept by faith and see the deliverance of the Lord.

Having experienced trials and temptations myself, I have come to experience God's power and his redeeming quality. The trials and temptations that I have faced have given me the opportunity to be a better person and spiritually mature.

God is always able and willing to deliver those who trust in him. By making the right choice when tempted, you will come out stronger than you were before. In Psalm 91, the Bible tells us, 'He who dwells in the shelter of the Most High will rest in the shadow of the almighty.' It goes on to express the security we have when you choose to make God (Most High) your dwelling place.

The Scripture says no harm will befall us; no disaster will come near our tent, for he will command his angels to guard us in all our ways. In verse 13, the psalm says we will even tread upon the lion and the cobra that will attack us. These are all those things that the Devil will want to use to threaten our lives, such as sickness, poverty, depression, shame and disgrace, betrayals, destruction, divorce, and separation.

The Devil magnifies problems so that the problems may look deadly to his target, but God says we will trample on the great lion and the serpent just because we choose to love the Lord.

The same psalm tells us that God says when we acknowledge his name he will rescue us and protect us. When we faced with trouble as a Christian, He will be with us, deliver us, and honour whatsoever we ask Him to do for us in times of trouble. At the end of all the trials, He will compensate us by satisfying us with long life and show us His salvation. Can you imagine that? Saving you will be his gift to you.

I have come to believe beyond doubt that the Word of God is in fact real and living just as God says in the Bible. I have gone through trials of many kinds/ and if it had not been for God, I do not know where I would have been. I thank God that though I became a born-again Christian at an early age/ I was able to prove beyond any reasonable doubt that Jesus is Lord! I am convinced, persuaded/ and content that nothing is impossible with God. Through him, all things are possible.

I saw the Lord delivers me and my parents and brothers and sisters from death. Death came to our door to threaten our lives in the form of 'rebels' during the civil war in Sierra Leone. It came in the form of heavily armed insurgents dressed up in army uniforms while holding guns and machine guns in army trucks never yet seen in my life. Disguised with evil and desperate to kill and to destroy, they called aloud for all the occupants in our home to come out and shot rapidly at our gated fence. soon we saw them, one after the other, jump out of their trucks and violently thump the gate.

At the face of death, when I imagined—as already told by some of our friends—young girls, were already raped and brutally killed. My heart fainted. I had already seen children holding guns and rampant looting taking place in our treasured community; enemies taking vengeance as a result of lawlessness The smell of death was horrible as it smell did not devour us. With our last hope, we cried out to the Lord and sought the face of God to deliver us from death, and miraculously these people suddenly left our front gate without any of us being hurt. They shouted as they went, 'We are coming back!' I tell you this: the Lord never permitted them to come back. **The lord rescued us.** The Lord rescued us. Lost in sea, when all hopes disappeared, were the rumbling thunder and lightning strikes consuming fire. God became the captain, and in the midst of hopelessness, he brought deliverance.

Following our escape from the visit of the vicious death squad, my sister Amy, received a phone call from her friend of the news that, there was a paid rescue boat at the high sea. Our dad arranged to dropped us off on the boat and settled our fees and then left us to God security in particular, not particularly sure were the boat was heading. During the boat, sealing at high sea the boat got lost. The Captain was confused and the whole passengers traumatised by the event on the boat without direction and instruction; as the boat overloaded with family to include young people, elderly women and children jam-packed on each other in the dark of the night at high sea. At one point, I became seasick and vomited and was afraid then began to pray like I have never done in my Christian life then. I also saw other Christian praying and I could remember as weak as I was, tried to preach the gospel to people nearby and they were willing and asking to give their lives to Jesus as their last resort of hope.

By this hour, we were, told the journey would be 24 hours has become three eventful and very fearful days on the high sea without specific direction. Suddenly, when all hopes disappeared, we were again, confronted by the rumbling thunder and lighten which consistently stroke like a consuming fire; God became the Captain of the boat and in the mist of hopelessness brought deliverance.

We heard the Boat Crew signalling that we were approaching the republic of the Gambia shone, and the weak, sick and the very frail people on the boat; very many us boarded the boat without food or drink and never eaten in days'. I myself looked so lean it has shocked me. People broke into tears, tears of joy and being alive and another hope of thanks given.

As we approach the port, just before the anchor, we could see from the dashboard of the boat where we were standing, several uniform men and women from the custom, members of Red Cross, Immigration and other anxiously waiting for us.

We were asked for our passport and I presented and also my sisters too went through the immigration checks and we were allow without difficulty into the Republic of the Gambia.

There in the Gambia the Lord set us apart for his work, though, lost, and displaced from our home, God provided and meet all our needs and we were favour in the mist of the Gambian people. In the Gambia, I saw youth from well respectable home from Sierra Leone went into prostitution and promiscuous life for survival. In all of this, the Lord diligently took care of us to the very end of our stay in the Gambia. My younger brother, sisters and I all had the opportunity to further our studies and are all alive and living.

In one afternoon, In the Gambia my mother was suddenly taken into emergency care. She suffer black out and could not breathe. Lay in the hospital bed motionless with no adequate diagnosis, there in the hospital bed I felt empathy for my dear mum, who I believe was taken ill due to thought of the lost and detriment she had suffer at that time. I was also frightened about the thought of death. My fear as the elder child there in the Gambia, was that were would I start if such thing was to happen. I was more concern about my siblings than I was, as they always believed that I know the answers to their entire questions for our future. What was I going to tell my little brother who once in his statement asked me a very interesting question.

As a young boy he did not understood the change, he was going through. The statement was "I don't like it here, why did we not take our big house with us when coming "There by the hospital bed looking at my motionless and beautiful mother I prayed an earnest prayer to God. I said 'Lord you said in your word that by your strips we were ill and that by you dying on the cross you took all our infirmities from us and nail them on the cross; if you save my mother I will not forget you for the rest of my life. If you could only make a sudden change in her despondent situation, I will serve you for the rest of my life.

I tell you this, the Lord save my mother and there was a sudden change in my mother's medical situation. We left the hospital with an able mum. O! to God be all the glory. My mother who I also later told us she prayed the same prayer that she may not die but live is now happily living in Sierra Leone with my dad were the Lord favoured them. The Lord gave them all the devil took from them. These are but a few of my 'testimonies' of the goodness of God in my life.

The Lord has constantly and continuously with me up to this hour in my life. Though there are constant battles, I have come to know the Lord with a new name 'The God of continuality'.

However, I could not have been so thankful today to the President of the Republic of the Gambia, His Excellency, President J.J.Jaymen and the entire people of the Gambia for the very way they helped us to temporary settle in the Gambia. The Gambia people, the Red Cross and the other volunteers' teams were very helpful and supportive by every circumstance, My foundation of Christianity is on Jesus, not on my pastors, great men of God, my parents, or money, but on Jesus. It is because of this foundation in Jesus—his grace, faithfulness, and abundance of love—that I can proudly say that I am still a believer in Jesus and a Christian after all these years. I can proudly say it is well with me and my future is secure in Jesus's name.

I must state that as a Christian, you must not be ignorant to the devices of Satan. Satan will do everything he can to keep you out of your faith as a born-again believer in God and to divert you from God. The Devil already knows his destiny, and he will use every possible distraction so we end up in the same place as him. This will not be in Jesus's name.

The Devil will use anything from discouragement, betrayals, and headaches to cancer and from poverty to wealth to distract you from heaven and fulfilling your divine purpose. You must not give up. The Devil will purposely bring people around whose aim is to destroy you. They work in jealousy and make secret plans of wickedness to harm you. These ones are the malicious friends that you are unaware. You must focus on Jesus and not on your circumstances or the people around you.

Getting prepared will enable you to move more boldly. People fall into temptations and fail because they fail to take time to equip themselves as Christians against the attraction of the world in which they live.

The Bible says that we are like sheep in the midst of wolves and that the Devil is like a roaring lion seeking those he may devour. He will roar to make you panic, but when you know your God and the power he has given you, you will be bold and not shaken.

The good news is that Jesus overcame the world on your behalf. Until you read the Bible and spend time in God's Word, you will not be able to apply the Word of God to your situation and you will not be able to identify things that are either from God or from the Devil. You will still be full of disobedience, anger, stress, and depression, to name but a few.

Every student who intends to pass an examination can only achieve success through consistent studying, which involves taking some time go through your notes and reading books so that he/she can pass the exam. The Bible tells us in Ephesians 8 that we must put on the whole armour of God. So that having gone through all trials, we will be able to stand. Jesus was in the wilderness for forty days and forty nights fasting and praying to prepare for what was ahead of him.

When you know that 'no weapon formed against you shall prosper and every tongue that will arise against you in judgement shall be condemned,' you will not spend your time stressing about your bullying boss who wants to abuse his position to get you sacked because you refused to cooperate in a conspiracy against another fellow worker or colleague. Nor will you spend your time crying over that woman or man threatening your marriage, but you will be in the position to know that they will surely not prosper.

Through preparation by learning how to put on the armour of God, you will be in the position to understand how to use the weapon of prayer to make your requests made known to God, knowing that they that are for you more than they that are against you. Whatsoever you asked the Lord in accordance with his Word, in the name of Jesus, should be so.

God can also prepare you for his will to be done in your life. God will allow certain trials and temptations to come your way so that he can prepare you for his blessing. God will want to bring out the giant in you so you can deal with the giant blessing that is coming your way.

It can sometimes be painful when going through certain trials and temptations in life, but never give in to the Devil. The Bible tells us that God will never allow you to be tempted with what you cannot handle. You have the ability to handle every trial and temptation that comes your way. No temptation has seized you except what is common to man. God is faithful; he will not let you be tempted beyond what you can bear. When you are tempted, he will also provide a way out so that you can stand up under it (1 Corinthians 10:13).

Do not be ignorant of the devices of the Devil. Study the Bible so that you can familiarise yourself with the tricks of the Devil. He has used the same strategy and old tricks since the foundation of the earth.

It is very interesting how some people react when you are going through trials in life. It is in trials that you will get to know those people who are truly your friends and loved ones. As the saying goes, 'Your best friend could be your greatest enemy.' This saying is definitely true.

There are those of your so-called best friends that will run away from you in trials. It could be painful, but take heart, for your new best friend is on the way. Some people do not need to be around you if you are to be successful in life—if you are to have an encounter with the Lord. They are like a storming block to you seeing the Lord. God has to remove them from your life so that they will not contaminate your blessings.

These people show you 'white teeth,' but their heart is dark towards you. They pretend to be your friend, but the content of their heart is full of evil desires towards you. So when these so-called friends betray you, count it as joy. God has just delivered you.

There may be people that like to be around you because they use you as a yardstick to measure their failures and successes. At times, they pretend to be that helping hand when you have problems, but deep inside their hearts, they are full of joy that you are having those problems.

Only, God knows the thoughts of all the people around you, even in our ignorance. That is why he will sometimes allow you to go through certain trials and temptations; this is so in order for him to shape and position you in the right place. He will shred all those people out of your life, all those that the Devil will use to devour your blessings.

Do not be dismayed when you get into a certain trial and some of your so-called friends begin to run away from you. It is not because you are a bad person but because your miracle is on the way, God has chosen you. You are only going through the test for you to get your testimony. Jesus says that he is a friend that sticks closer than a brother does. He will never leave you alone—this, is the unfailing love and faithfulness we have in Jesus.

Have you ever wondered how certain people have a word of advice for you only when you are facing problems? They seem to have all the answers to your mistakes, failures, and reasons why you went into that mess in the first place; but as soon as you are on your feet, they seem to be unhappy and you wonder why. It is because they were happier when your life was, wrought with problems. You wonder why the sudden changes. Yes, they enjoy the position of supposedly comforting you during difficult times, but really, they enjoy it and want you to stay there.

Overcoming your problems threatens their personal evil desire for you. I say this because of personal experience and I am here to encourage you: when all is lost, hold on to Jesus and never give up or give in. Trust in the Lord. He will do it for you and see it through. Where others fail, you will succeed. No matter how messed up your life is, God can and will fix it for you. Your head must never bow down because as Christians, born of God, we have been, risen up with Jesus and are more than a conqueror. We must carry ourselves like winners. Your finished person will wonder many of what God has done in your life. If you told, you will probably not have believed it. This is the power of God working in us.

True Love in Jesus

True love will always embrace you in time of trouble. God sometimes needs to show you that man cannot be trusted. You cannot put your trust in man; God needs you to totally dependent on him. He needs to teach you that your bread comes from heaven and that even when man will not feed you, He is able to, and will, provide for you.

He provided manna for the children of Israel and fed Elijah with bread through the ravens. Have you ever wondered how the trees in the forest grow or the birds in the air feed themselves? It is the perfect work of God. What more is that it is you that he calls his son? If he can do that for ordinary birds in the air, he will definitely do it for you. This is why you have to be prepared so that when trial comes, you will be comforted and not give up.

See, as evil as man is, we lie, kill, steal and does all manner of sinful act still we know how to give good food to our children. What can us than say about God? He will by no means allow the wickedness of the Devil to prosper in our life. Christ's love is powerful; he touches the lives and meets the need of whosoever will call upon him. One thing I personally liked about Jesus is that I can be myself with him. I can freely express myself in a way I will not necessary do to others. This is because I know he loves me dearly. I also know that Jesus cannot come all the way from heaven and die for my sins just to neglect me because of one silly mistake. The Bible tells us that God has loved us with an everlasting love. This kind of love is perfect and there is no fear in it. The beginning and the end sealed by the blood of Jesus and cannot changed by anything.

God loves us more than we even love ourselves. Jesus Christ wants to give you eternal life. He also wants to give you a quality life here on earth and to be an existing part of your daily living. He wants to bear your daily burdens and give you peace.

Jesus is the master of forgiveness. He can forgive and forget, and He can cast out Satan in your life and set you free from every demonic power and oppression of the Devil. He has the ultimate power to forgive and to deliver. The Bible says in the book of James that mercy overcomes judgement. Therefore, the mercies of God in your life overcome all judgement of the Devil over your life.

When you become born again, there are challenges that you are likely to face, which may likened to that of Job. They could be from errors you may make or that of other people around you. On the other hand, from conflict of interest among family members, on the train, in your work life, as a member of group (whether Christian or non-Christian) or members of the public.

There are such problems that will arise at one point or the other in your life that will test your faith and the strength of your belief in Christ. This is why the Bible admonished us to be alert and to assured in the love we have in Jesus.

The expectation of Christ in this situation is not to be reactionary, to act on impulse, but to see Christ through the problems and the difficulties by addressing the situation through honest due diligence and consistencies with the Word of God, holding up to your faith, and waiting on the Lord without waiving your stands in the matter. Even if no one agrees with you or with the position, you hold. This is because our God is not a God of 'The Majority' but a God of love, truth, favour, and peace.

This is the image of our God. Through calmness in any situations, that troubles us. If only we obey the principle of God's love that tells us his plan for us is not to destroy us or to be afraid but to set us free. This is reaffirming by the Scriptures that he will be faithful to the end even if we make genuine mistake.

Now the issue of building and establishing your relation with Jesus is a very serious matter; one that needs to be dealt with by every Christians. I say serious because, failing to do so will have severe effect in your journey and walk with God. It will, if you are not careful cause you to backslide and miss heaven. I want to encourage you to invest in your time with God by getting into the scriptures and allowing the Holy Spirit to control everything about you. Remember, it is all about Jesus.

I have an attitude of taking note during sermon time in church services, conferences, seminars and where ever the word of God is been taught or preached. I learnt this at a very early stage in my 'born again' life. I will take note to enable me to do a thorough bible study on my own. I use the same study skills learnt in the classroom and apply it to the study of the word of God. I do so to confirm whether what I had subjected myself to or hear is indeed in line with the word of God and to give me a better understanding of the scripture guided by the Holy Spirit. I sometimes uses different version of the bible to enable me get a better interpretation for my—personal understanding.

Every one born into this world is in a solo journey and this journey is a test for eternity life. The bible tells us that we must study to show ourselves approved (2 Timothy 2:15). Just as with every examination, we can either pass or fail. This is why we need to study the word of God so we can know how to pass the test at the end of our journey on earth and make it to heaven. In the case of our Christian work, Jesus took the exam, on our behalf. He passed the test with perfect distinction; all you have to do is, to be in one with Jesus. Become a part of the body of Christ. You become one with Jesus only when you are 'born again' (please read chapter one for more information on how to be 'born again'). If you can do that, then, you have acquired the revelation to eternal life—heaven. You are sure to pass the test of life.

However, the devil does not want you to make it to Heaven and so he is in the business of making people fail. Sadly as it might be the devil start in the church. There are all sorts of behaviours in the church that discourage believers to backslide and I believe those people who will backslide because of some of the challenges they find in the church is due to their lack of good foundation in Jesus. In their failing, sadly they are wholly responsible for their life. Scripture says my people (Gods people—Christians or born again) are perish because of lack of knowledge. (Hosea 4:6)

I am going to deal with this matter as observed in the church today and I hope both those who are responsible for some of the things dealt with hear will find in their godly heart to change and begin to act like a true Christian. I pray we as Christian should take conscious steps to address ourselves in the way we comport ourselves as born again Christian and stop blaming the devil for all the bad behaviours in the church. There has never been a time for change as such a time like this.

If you however, think you are a victim of bad mannered influences in the church; if your Christian life is been deteriorated because of one appalling scenario in the church please, read this chapter very seriously and I pray the Holy Spirit will help you in your way back to Jesus. Remember, your salvation is in Jesus and the purpose of your being is about Jesus and nothing to do with anyone; not on your pastors or any other persons. I implore you take your time to invest in your relationship with Jesus and build a solid foundation in Him.

As many and as different as we are so is our purpose and reasons for going to church. I will like to emphasis on the reason in line with the word of God—to worship and to fellowship. When we go to the house of the Lord, we go to worship and to fellowship with God. As Christian, we are commanded by God to observe the Lords day. (Exodus 20:8). When we become a Christian, God faithfully called us into a relationship with Him (1 Corinthians 1:9).

We are to establish a relationship by fellowship first with God then, with other Christians. (1 John 1:3). Fellowship means companionship, friendship, bond to name but a few. Therefore, we must come as we are. We must come not be shame and hid our sin before God but, be free in our mind, body and soul. Am blessed to have experience companionship and friendship and there are things I will tell my companion that I will not tell any other person. I feel free to talk to my husband in a way I will not talk to a man in my church. This is how God want us to be with him—free.

God never gives up on us so we must not give up on ourselves, or be shame to come to him just as you are. He knows our problems and he is willing and ready to help. We talk to God when we pray. When you go into prayer to talk to God, go just as you are in the sense that, you tell him your heart felt feeling about your concerns. If am anger with someone for hurting me, I come to God and tell him. I say 'Lord, I am not God, I am anger because of this or that and honestly I cannot find myself to forgive, but since you are God do your miracle in me,' if upset I say 'Lord am upset'. I do so because I know like David I cannot deceive God. David said 'If I rise on the wings of the dawn, if I settle on the far side of the sea' God is always there so we cannot hide from God. (Psalm 139:9). I call my sin by its name.

When you practise to call your sins by it name before God there is nothing to be ashamed of before ordinary humans. Do not paint your sins with beautiful colour to please yourself or use grammar to sugar coat your sins; do you think you can speak your language more than God can? God is the author of our languages and he is the one that put our languages in our mouth.

We pretend in the church because of the attitude of the Christian in the church. We are afraid of rejection and being different. We are concern about what people will think of us. I tell you different is good. Being different attract Gods attention. There is no need to pretend and God knows and sees our every moves. It is better for you to settle it with God than to be pleasers of man. Paul says in Galatians 1:10 we are not call to please people or the approval of people but as servant of Christ.

The devil wants you to hide because he wants you to die in your sin, so he makes you to think that you will be dome if you are to tell someone. He put you in the position where you will feel shame, so instead of you to seek Gods face you backslide; but nothing that takes your liberty from you is from God. Scripture says, "If the Son sets you free, you will be free indeed". (John 8:36). You need this freedom of John 8:36 therefore I huge you to change your conceptions by building your God found relationship.

God does not want you to be ashamed or feel guilt or condemnation. These things are not from God, why should God put those things on you when He took then form us. God took all our shame and guilt and he nail them on the cross. He is faithful to forgive you all the time. In light to the 'rebels' I mentioned earlier—if they are alive and happen to be reading this book right now, I want to pray with them, and I would like them to pray the prayer of repentant in chapter 1.

In addition, like David prayed in Psalm 51:10, pray that God will recreate in you a new heart and renew a right spirit within you and see how God's deliverance will come upon you. In true repentance, one can find undeserved forgiveness and love from God through Jesus Christ that surpasses human understanding. I also encourage anyone reading this book in need of forgiveness and love to do so in Christ Jesus, and you will receive peace of heart.

If God is for you who can be against you?

The bible tells us in the book of Job that when the angels assemble to God to give report of the happenings on earth, Satan the accuser also went and presented himself. (Job1) While God was commending Job he boasted of Job his servant, the Devil gave spiteful comment. God boasted of Job because he was a righteous man and he feared the Lord. The devil stated that Job's wealth, riches was the reason of his love for God. God had blessed Job, he prospers him for he was a man who fear and love God.

The Devil comment on the beautiful children and friends and families God gave Job. There were blessing all around Job. The devil challenged God that if God was to take all those things form Job, Job will curse God and die. In Job chapter 1and 2 we see Satan the accuser of believer rebellious argue with God. He challenges Job's purpose for fearing God. He doubts Job's honest principles of life.

Job suffers great loss for being a righteous man who feared the Lord with all his heart. This was the devil trying to prove God's wrong about Job, Satan removes Job's wealth and health; all at almost the same time.

In reading the book of Job, I tried to reason with Job. This man was certain that he was a righteous man, and wondered why he was going through the kind of agony he was going through but, those whom he trusted, those that use to dine with him, whom he had faith in were the ones whose chastisement he felt the most. The people whom he thought would reason and believe him had doubt in him. They asked question like 'How can God punish a righteous person'. They were sure that Job must have some hidden sin only know by God.

It is very sad when a Christian relates suffering to sin and prosperity to righteousness. Misery is not necessarily, prevented by how religious we are, or base on our religious observance. When faced with suffering as a Christian of any kind, we must not stop believing in God or 'quit the religion'. It could be that God is boasting of you like Job. At this time, it is wise if you could seek God face.

During trials is when you hold steadfast to God and tarry before the throne of grace, so even if it is the devil trying to disprove your motive in serving God the Devil will fall. At this time, you get closer to God like you have never been before. One thing is for sure, our God reigns over all the earth. Your life is in God's hands and only God have the final say of your destiny.

Perhaps God is boasting of you today, how would you respond? When everything seem to be hopeless and lost and help seen to be no were to be found; what do you do. You do like Job. Clinging on God your maker, Job is there as an example for you to learn and to know that God will reward you beyond you can asked or imagine. You should focus on Him and not to your trails and temptations.

Do you really love God?

In trials, you will know those who really love the Lord. In trials, that you will know those who also love you. Job was a successful man before he went into his trailing period or wilderness. He must have got many friends. Scripture says that his children party a lot.

All his family and relatives would have been proud of him because of his previous wealth and success. But none of them were found or mentioned in the bible that they actually came to help or render assistance to Job except the three that came to mourn with him. Although they were of little help as they went in hypocrisy.

I am sure Job's friends fled from him the instant he became poor with all his trouble. They did not want to identify themselves with him because of his condition. His wife whom should have been his last resort of hope advised him to curse God and die. Job also suffered agony and pain.

The worse is his nightmare at night time, when his entire accuser was gone and left he alone, when he could at least have some sleep he was also, chastised with awful dreams and nightmares. Can you imagine that? However, the bible also tells us that in the end Job came out stronger than he uses to be. The bible tells us that the latter days of Job's life were greater than the beginning.

What can any man say to Job now, nothing but to honour him for his greatness. The bible tells us that God gave Job seven times seven of all he lost and the bible tells us that: the beauty of Jobs daughter was not to found on the faces of the earth. Can you beat that? What a wonder working God we serve.

This is what happens when you know your God and trust in him. When you fear God and honour him with your life. God will never forsake you nor will he allow the devil to kill you with your problems. He always has a plan to deliver you and to bless you for your troubles.

These lessons such as Job's, are all in the bible to help us learn and to teach us how to act when we are faced with such problems. By reading your bible its helps us to be equipped should we have such battles to fight in our own life.

It is very necessary that you get prepared. In fact, the more you grow and get closer to God the more Satan will try to attack or tempt you.

He will study your every move and knows your full name by heart. But don't lose hearts; the grace of God is in abundance and Jesus overcame him on your behalf. The battle was over when Jesus died on the cross and rose again from the grave over 2000 years ago. Jesus said in John 16:33 "..I have overcome the world". The devil is fighting a losing battle while your name will be remembered in heaven.

In preparing yourself should you are face with any trial or temptations, you have to study the word of God yourself, pray boldly. Prayer is a deadly weapon to the devil. The devil will do everything to stop you from praying, but be strong and ready to fight the battle, knowing that they that are for you are more than the devil and all the forces of darkness put together.

Our mind can be very vulnerable at a point of suffering. Trials and temptations and the devil will want to attack your mind. When he begins to put thoughts of condemnation in your heart, don't stop praying but continue, resist him and he will flee from you.

If you refuse to be intimidated by the devil; you will not be moved by his treats. The devil is nothing but an "uncircumcised Philistines". If you know the story of David and Goliath, you will know what happen to Goliath the "Uncircumcised Philistines" who stood before the army of God's people cursing them. His head was cut off by the young man of God call David who believed in his God.

I will at this point encourage you to invest in a bible or teaching tapes and practices to confess positive things in your life. Cut out those friends that do not edify the Lord. No matter who you are, as bad company corrupt good character so likewise; Birds of the same fathers flocks together'.

You will surely face trails and temptation. The devil will wrestle with your imaginations and thoughts, your emotions and everything he can gets hold of. Through discouragement, rejections from people whom you had confide in, your friends and in some case your love ones. As human you will be emotionally derange but you must learn to focus your problems on Jesus and not on the problems.

When you begin to spend time focusing on your problems, you magnify it. It becomes bigger and bigger and will begin to boast like Goliath. But when you resist it, and focus on Jesus through reading your bible, prayer, worship, and listening to the word of God. Faith will come.

By faith in Jesus you can bring down any mountain in your life. Only be positive and trust in God, think positive things, say positive words like" this too must pass" "With God all things are possible" yes! Jesus loves me" find out what the bible says about your circumstance and believe in the report of the Lord. Refuse to be defeated, know your God and do not accept failures to determine your future. In doing so, you will come out a winner.

With God on your side you will come out stronger so that when God began to use you or entrust thousands in your hands, you will be in the position to appreciate him and use your talent well. Your friends will criticized you, they will say "is this not so and so with no formal education, that holds that position" know that your qualification is from above, and that when God qualifies you, no one can disqualify you.

Set your heart on Jesus, honour and listen to him. Try and do your own part, to the best of your ability and God will take it from there. God will prepare you in whatever way he chooses.

If God needs to prepare you to speak before kings and queens he will provide the education and give you the boldness to do it. If God wants you to have self-control and patience he will put you in the mist of the difficult people you can ever imagine so he can perfect you in those areas.

God sometimes develop real peace within us not by making things go the way we have planned but allowing times of chaos and confusion to come our way then give us the peace Jesus demonstrated in the bible. We learn real peace by choosing to trust God in circumstances in which we are tempted to worry or be afraid. May the peace of God and the sweet fellowship of the Holy Spirit be with you now and forever Amen!

Understanding temptations

According to Wikipedia, the free encyclopaedia "Temptation is the desire to perform an action that one may enjoy immediately or in the short term but will probably later regrets for various reasons: legal, social, psychological (including feeling guilt), health-related, economic, etc.

'In the context of religion, temptation is the inclination to sin. Temptation also describes the coaxing or inducing a person into committing such an act, by manipulation or otherwise of curiosity, desire or fear of loss.'

In this chapter I have made a little emphasis on temptation to defer it from trials. While trails can sometimes be conducted by God, God can never tempt a person and God cannot be tempted with evil. From the above definition we see a person desire to perform an action is the foundation of been tempted. Temptation is not seduction, anything that you have strong desire to do that opposes God, that leads to sin according to scripture is temptation.

Temptation is nothing but a plan to sin. It instigate one to do something wrong and can comes to us as a thought in our mind. Temptation can also come to us from what we hear, see, feel, or even as a suggestion direct from the devil. The devil can put such thoughts into our mind to lure us into sin. There are lots of things that can incite or tempt us to sin. Yielding to temptation will causes one to sin against God.

You must understand that God cannot tempt you with evil. God cannot tempt you at all. We are tempted by our own evil desire by accepting the thoughts and ideas of the devil. The bible tells us in James 1:13 *"When tempted, no one should say, "God is tempting*

me." For God cannot be tempted by evil, nor does he tempt anyone;"
James1:13.

No one is exempted from been tempted but how you manage your temptations is what makes the difference. You must not think that you have sinned just because you have been tempted. As a Christian the devil knows that we are of Christ, and his plans to kill, steal and to destroy us has fail so he always come with one thing or the other to find a way to turn us back from the protection we have in Jesus.

Although Trail and temptation are different, however, the two can go together. That is, your temptations can be a trial. I would like to tell you that temptations can be overcome. God has put the power to overcome temptation in you. We received that power when we became born again.

In the book of Matthew chapter 4:1-11 we see that Jesus was tempted by the devil after Jesus had fasted for forty days and forty nights. Jesus was a man. He walk and talk like a man. He suffer, hungered, thirsted as a man and was also tempted as a man, yet without sin (Hebrews 4:15). Jesus knew what it meant to be tempted with sin and the things of this world. That why he died on the cross for you and I so we can be perfected in Him. Through him we received the power to resist temptation.

Having fasted for such period of time the bible said Jesus was hungry. Our body needs food to continue living. At the end of Jesus fasting, the body would have been crying for food. The devil knowing that, decided to seize the opportunity to tempt Jesus, but he fail woefully. Why? This was not because Jesus was a superman but because Jesus knew the word of God.

Jesus feared and has faith in the scripture. He said "It is written". Matthew 4:4. We see in Verse seven Jesus resist the devil while he spoke the word of God *"Away from me, Satan! For it is written: ..."* the bible tell us that the devil left Jesus after Jesus resisted or rebuke the devil; and angels came and attend to him. When you resist the devil he will flee from you. He cannot do anything beyond your will.

He simply does not have the power to do so. By you commanding the devil to depart from you, you create a place for the Holy Spirit. You will received more power and reward from God.

Jesus uses the word of God to overcome his temptation. The Scriptures are there to teach us Good from Evil. If what you are about doing, thinking, seeing or hearing is against the word of God it's wrong and will lead you to sin. You not always remember that the wages of sin is death but the gift of God is eternal life. We can see that there are two result of temptation and each brings different consequences. Yield to temptation, we sin against God. Reject temptation, we become spiritually stronger!

We learn in the previous chapter that we must count it all joy when we are face with all kinds of trials and temptations. James 1:1-3. When you are face with trials and temptations it makes you stronger they are steps to the unfailing blessings and destiny of God in your life. You experience the grace of Christ. It is often said there is no testimony without a test. It is only after you go through the test that you can have a testimony. The challenges are therefore will be a stepping ground for your blessings.

As Christian I must emphasise that we must not spend time in been religious with the devil. The devil is an expert in what he does and he has lived long before you can imagine. The temptation you might be tempted with by the devil might be new to you but, it's an old story to the devil, he has over a hundred ways to tempt you to derive into one conclusion—to sin against God. You will be wasting your precious time in making conversation with the devil. If it takes you to flee like Joseph flee from Potiphar's wife in the book of Genesis 39 then do it. But don't engage with the devil. The devil is a liar and the father of all lies so we must not do or act as he direct us.

For example, it is very tempting to do harm when provoke to madness but doing the madness does not prevent you from suffering the consequences of your action. Likewise, lack and poverty does not justify burglary. There is always a way to do otherwise. Therefore, self-control is an important 'fruit of the Sprit' that a Christian should have. (Galatians 5:22-23)

Self-control will prevent you from covetousness, hatred, excessive hanger, stealing to name but a few, these are some of the features or devices that the devil uses to tempt us.

When you find yourself in a room with a woman or man whom you are attracted to, and you begin to touch each other, do not spend time binding the devil. Remove yourself from the room and get away. If it takes you to run, then do it. There is no crime in doing that. There is no amount of binding that will stop you from eventually, committing fornication or adultery if you remain and try to play spiritual. You can do the binding later.

I have seen Christians who want to know everything about anything and are ever so interested in everyone's business. They are always available to listen to gossip about anyone. People feel very free to discuss about others to them and in their present. They always seem to, accidentally find themselves in the gathering of gossipers.

Such people should not blame the devil when they hear gossip of themselves, because what goes around comes around. In this case you will get more than the measure you sow. what they need to do is to channel their time into something profitable and useful. Failing to do that, in due course will lead them to problems that will build a barrier to their Christian growth.

Personally I hate gossiping and despise been in the mist of people who sit down to talk about others in a malicious way for whatever reason. I see it as a complete waste of time; not to mention the amount of negative energy that involves in it. I call it an act of witchcraft. When I became born again, I began to study my bible I was ever so happy to know that it is a blessing for one not to seat among mockers but delight in the meditation of the word of God. (Psalm1).

All these things can be tempting and differ from one person to another. As previously said the devil has a million ways to tempt a person but for the transforming believer I have brought these points so you can think about these things and for you to be aware and be alert should the devil tempted you.

Remember the word of God is the most powerful tool to overcoming temptation. Do not think about the temptation rather upon the word of God and you will find yourself naturally overcoming your temptations.

Prayer as a weapon

Prayer is a tool use to achieve supernatural things in your life. As a Christian the bible says *2 Corinthians 10: 4-5* *"For the weapons of our warfare are not carnal but mighty in God for pulling down strongholds, ⁵ casting down arguments and every high thing that exalts itself against the knowledge of God, bringing every thought into captivity to the obedience of Christ"*

Its empower you to become stronger and to release your mind from stress and give you peace of mind. Prayer is a way of getting into the present of God.

Every Christian ought to live a devotional prayer life. In Mathew 6:6 Jesus talked about prayer as having a private time with God. This type of prayer is talking about having intimacy with God. Prayers cause you to have a relationship with God; this is because in prayer you communicate with God. God hear your prayers and he respond to you. You gain experience when you live a prayerful live. Until you pray and see your prayers answered, you will not experience the power of prayer.

Prayer is also a great weapon to fight trials and temptations in your life. With prayers, you can change situation and move mountain. When you are face with a trialling situation, you should know that, it is time for advancement in your spiritual growth and maturity. I love prayer and I do a lot of it. I adore the bonding and quality time that comes in spending my time praying in God's presence. I can be myself with God in prayer. I tell Him all the good, bad and ugly and have confident that am still safe with Him.

I can only imagine what it will be like on that glorious day when I shall see Jesus; His glory, Holiness the might of His overwhelming love and power. Down on my kneel praying in a trialling time. I had experience the power of the presence of the Holy Spirit in my life. It came upon me in a peaceful, gentle and calm manner. I felt an overwhelming love in my heart, as he comforted me. At that time, I was certain that God has answered my prayers.

A trial usually comes with changes. Change of lifestyle, obligations, power, authority and more. In other for you to step into these changes and be an overcomer, you must also make some changes in your life to adopt into these changes. When you are face with a trial do not sit back and expect it to go away just because you are a child of God. As a child of God, the devil can defeated you if, you do not work as a child of God. Your problems will boast on you and even threaten your life. Lazarus was a friend of Jesus but he still died. He was, raised from the dead only when his sisters interceded on his behalf and called on Jesus. Your problems will not go away by magic; instead, it will magnify itself when you sit down expecting God to come from heaven to say the magic word. Your trial and temptation calls for changes, so act accordingly.

When your situation calls for a change so is your prayer life. You should pray like you have never prayed before, and pray yourself into position to received Gods divine intervention in your situation.

Your prayer pattern should also change, if you are used to praying with your heads down and in your understanding, it is time to begin to pray with your heads up and with the prayer of the Holy Spirit; that is, opening your mouth and say something. Refuse defeat by your enemy the devil. If it takes, you to make a fool of yourself like the blind men in Mathew chapter 20 then do it.

The bible says when Jesus was passing by. Two blind men heard that Jesus was passing by. They were blind and therefore could not see

Jesus. I believe there were others, who were strong and able, whom they could not compete with physically but they also knew that the only way that they can get the attention of Jesus in that crowd is to shout the name of Jesus, so they did. Now, there were people of high calibre whom considered there shouting as an embarrassment and one that lack dignity. Nevertheless, the bible tells us that the blind men shouted, the more, they said Jesus! Son of David have mercy on us. They had considered their situation, they knew how hard it is to be blind, and were desperate for a change. As they were not prepared, for the devil to stop them from receiving their blessings nor did, they want to remain the same so they shouted even more. The bible tells us that because they made a fool of themselves and shouted the more, Jesus stopped and answered to their calling. He said, "What do you want me to do for you".

If only you could dear to make a 'fool' of yourself, Jesus will come into your life to give you what you desire. You might have got everything in your life but there is that one thing that you so desire that the devil had bounded you form having, so that you will never be happy. Maybe it is a child, or marriage or even that promotion in your office or forgiveness that you so desire but you have not received it.

You have tried so long and have done everything in your power to come out of the situation but fail. The devil is aware of all the patterns and steps you have taken to overcome this pain, because it has been there for so long. Now is the time to change your pattern of doing things and do something different and radical that will even surprise the devil himself. Begin to pray differently, shout if you have never shouted before. When you pray and make a fool of yourself regardless of what people may think or say, you will surely court the attention of God and he will surely come to your rescue. He will say to you son/daughter what do you want me to do for you.

One thing that the Lord thought me, he said, if you can trust me enough to go about living your life as if you are not going through any problem; I will show you my deliverance according to his loving kindness. So any time am face with an unusually situation after praying and doing every other things to be done, I will begin to praise the Lord and thank him for his grace to delivered.

As Christian, we are call into a level of faith, because, our assignment on earth is great. Prise is the highest form of prayer. When you praise God, you agree to his word concerning your situation. You agree that which he said he will do; you confirm your faith in God—an expression of your gratitude.

The bible said that God inhabited our praise. (Psalm 22:3) To inhabit is to: tenanted, colonised. It is to settle and occupied meaning by praising God; we cause God's Sprit to come and live with us and in the presence of God, there is liberty. (2 Corinthians 3:17). Prise brings alive what is dead; because it moves God to action. It has empowered one to receive a miracle. Praise denotes simple faith and confident in God and faith never disappoint. You can praise your way into God present. Psalm 104:4.

Chapter 4

The principles of God

God is not a respecter of persons and the principles of God will never change. God respect principles. The more you learn and understand the principle of the bible the better it will be for you. As I am writing this I am still learning to apply the principles of God and by revelation, God is revealing new things to me every time. However, you do not need to know the entire bible to understand the principles of God. Learn as you grow. For every question asked, there is an answer, the answer sometime given by revelation from God.

Have you ever wondered why some people who are not born-again sometimes are very prosperous? We sometimes tried to take comfort by saying that God wants them to live longer so that they might have time to repents, true but, have you also considered that these people might in fact working in the principles of God. They have reaped what they had sowed. Let take for example, in principle everything that goes up must come down. When you add two to two in Africa it equal to four and so it is in America and the rest of the continent. There are so many principles of God, which you will come to know and understand by reading and studying the word of God. The Holy Spirit is our teacher who knows the very thought of God.

Learn to depend on the Holy Spirit and he will teach you great things from God that can only come by revelation. The bible tells us that the words of God are ye and Amen. It also says that the heavens and the earth will pass away but the words of God will remain. We must therefore understand that the principles of God does not apply only to the born again Christian but to all Gods creations. In this book, we will only elaborate the select principles of God as outline. I have chosen these selected because I believe every born again Christian should be mindful of them. I have briefly include this chapter but I implore you to read further to educate yourself and be knowledgeable of your calling as a Christian so you will not perish.

Long life

The bible tells us in Exodus 20:12 *'Honour your father and your mother, so that you may live long in the land the lord your God is giving you.'* that when we honour our father and mother, we will have long life. This scripture confirms the word of God. In other words being rude and disobedient to your parents decreases your life span. This also extended to people who are older than you are. The bible tells us in that: in the last days perilous times may come, children will be disrespectful to their parents; this is why the life span of man has reduced.

Imagine, in the days of Abraham, the bible tells us that people lived over a thousand of years. Children were very respectful of their fathers, and work in the fear of God always, so they lived long.

In this 21st century, we are seeing all manner of sin; children have no respect for their parent least alone the elder. So we see how disobedient and sin has cause us our life span been reduce by God. When you call yourself a born again Christian and you are disobedient and disrespectful to your parent and those who are older than you, know that you are violating the principle of God and expect the consequences. There is no if or buts about the matter. You may say but my parent does not deserve my respect, for one reason or the other; but God's principle does not change to fit our circumstances or personal conceptions. Now that you are born again, God has given you the power to change your destiny. God has given us the truth which is the word of God and it is the truth that will set us free.

If you are however, struggling with disobedient to your parent, I want to encourage you to repent of that sin and asked God to sanctify and empower you to begin to live an obedient life. It is for this very reason that Jesus died for you. Take it to the lord in prayer and ask God for forgiveness. Try everything you can, to start been obedient and ask the Holy Spirit to help you. God sees your effort and heart; he will give you the power to overcome your situation.

Marriage

Marriage is a constitution of God, the bibles tell us a man shall leave his family and cling to his wife. I Corinthians 1:13 says what God has joint together let no man put asunder. God loves and honour marriage, so likewise we ought to treat marriage with respect. There are certain blessings that come with marriage. The way we conduct ourselves in our marriage home, will either bring blessings or curses.

I have gone through my own fair share of marriage bliss and agony and believe I am in the position to write about this matter for the purpose of the transforming believer.

God loves marriage, he officiated the first marriage between a man and a woman in the Garden of Eden. *Genesis 2:24 "For this reason a man will leave his father and mother and be united to his wife, and they will become one flesh".*

This scripture refers to Adam and Eve in the book of Genesis (In the beginning). No families had existed before Adam and Eve. They were the first man and woman on earth. Why did God mention father and mother? It was a prophetic statement from God. God was saying 'this is how it will be' in the next verse, Genesis 2:25 the bible says "Adam and his wife . . .". Therefore marriage was part of the creation of God.

I want you to know that the devil is against marriage. The devil is also working actively to stop people to go into marriage and to destroy marriages. The devil hates you as a child of God. He also hates God and wants to destroy anything that God loves. He knows if he destroys marriage it will not please God, so he seeks to do just that. The devil does not want you to prosper in marriage. He hates a happy marriage. Now that you know this, I want to encourage you to be more cautious how you perceive your marriage and asked God to take over your marriage. Seek God in prayer to protect your marriage at all times so you will not fall into the devils evil plans.

God has place special blessings in the bed and home of a marriage couple. Whatever you agree in prayer as a couple it shall be done. This is a principle of God (Praying together and in agreement, *Mathew 18:18-20.)* This is why it is very important to seek God's face in choosing our partners before going into a marriage relationship. If you chose the devil for a wife or husband you will reap the fruit of the devil.

I personally do not think it is advisable for any person to go into marriage without seeking Gods help, cancelling and genuine love for each other. In this age we are living, we see divorce cases are just increasing by the minuet. This is the work of the devil to increase sin and eventually death. People go into marriages for every reason expects love and without involving God. When everything fails in a marriage or a relationship, it is only God and love that will be left.

Where there is love, there is a way and when love disappoints you, God will never fail. When the honeymoon period has pass, and the true colours of the flesh began to show up, it is only those marriages that are made in the love of God that will stand.

The truth is, whenever human beings are put to live together, there is bound to be personality differences. People are subject to change, in the case of marriages, two people of different background and different characters are united together with the purpose to live as husband and wife "till death do us part." It is natural that the very things that initially attracted you to your partner could be the worst behaviour you can't put up with when living together. At this point is when the devil comes in like a worm, to penetrate into those small areas and using His strategies of lies and deception to lure you away from the blessings of God and you permanently destroy you.

The devil who is the father of deception has always use deception to deceive God children. The devil will put conflict of interest in your marriage to destroy it like the fight of domination and leadership. There is a parable that says "no two captains cannot rule a ship". In the case of a marriage God has given the position of leadership to the man. The women he refers to as a 'help mate'. (I must emphasis a wife is not the same as a slave and vis visa). When a man fails to take his leadership position in the home there is a problem. The only alternative is for the woman to take leadership position and when this happens, you know you are in for a good fight.

As a preacher once said to the male he addresses, women are natural in the business of multiplication. You give a woman love; she will multiply it and produce babies. Give her a penny and she will increase your earning and added to it she will provide the finest meal for you. Give her security and you will never be troubled. But when a man gives a woman stress she will produce distress and give her tension she product hypertension for her husband.

My advice to men is that you tried to keep your wife happy by seek help form the lord and the sky will be your limit. Let her feel that she has a friend in you and you will get an everlasting friendship in her.

Because the devil oppresses marriage he tried to do everything he can to destroy it. Trials and temptation are not exempted in marriage but remember it is how you decided to deal with the matter that determines your victories.

All marriage couples battle with some kinds of trial at one point or another in their marriage. If you are reading this book and you are going through a marriage problem know that; you are not the only one who is or have gone through this battle, so cheer up. The important thing is the way we choice to react to these differences that will make or destroy our marriages or relationships. When we address our marriages according to God ways, we become secure in Gods promises. Gods plan for you is that you will have a happy marriage hear on earth. So when your husband/wife began to act crazy do not pack your bags and live, pray him/her into position.

Remember we "wrestle not against flesh and blood but against principality and powers" The devil is against marriages and he is doing everything he can to increase divorce case. When it gets too touch for you to handle, don't be ashamed to talk to a Christian friend who you know you can trust and who can pray with you. Do not seek the advice of a "desperate housewife" or you will get the reward of a "desperate housewife" Just keep obeying God on your side.

In my experience I have learnt to obey God in my own side. As you obey God as to whom you are in the marriage, God will intervene on your behalf and will reposition your partner to act accordingly.

It could be difficult if you think that you are the only one putting all the efforts in making things work and nothing seems to work. You will spend your time in stress, and operate in unforgiveness, anger, intolerant and more. If you are not careful you will get ill and by the time you know it you will not even know yourself; but when you take the entire burden to God in prayer he will give you peace in the mist of all the troubles.

Forgiveness is a powerful tool to use in fighting the devil to save your relationship in marriage. The 23rd Palms teach us the act of forgiveness, says, "for give us lord as we forgive others" a beautiful heart will come from the power of a forgiven heart. I have train myself not to work in un-forgiveness. This is because I am overwhelmed and full of God's love in my life. I have come to understand that it was while I was still a sinner that Christ dies for me, and not because of my righteousness. This does not mean that you should not get angry when offended, but means that you should not go to bed in bitterness so that you will not sin against God. Make a consciences decision to choice to be happy no matter what. Ask the Holy Spirit to embrace you with his love and he will.

There was a time in my relationship with my husband when I decided to move out, I wanted him out of my life and I was determined to do so. I blame him for everything and anything and verse versa. I was sowing discouragement, un-forgiveness, and argument and so on. It was not until I began to seek God for his purpose in my life and, when the love of God became stronger in me that I realise I have not been doing it Gods way. God told me about his principle of seed, time, harvest. You will reap whatever you sow.

You cannot sow tomatoes and expect to reap rice in time. You cannot sow yam and reap apple, when you sow tomatoes, you will reap tomatoes in time. I began to sow kindness, love, passion, forgiveness and all what I wanted from my husband. I began to pray my husband into position. Whenever we are together, I will put my hands on his head and bless him. I will say things to him that he had not heard from me for a very long time. As I began to honour God in been that Christian woman he want me to be, my relationship with my husband began to grow, and even though we have been together for 10 years, with all our ups and downs we can still say "I love you" and it will mean the same way, as when we first fell in love. It's amazing, it's a miracle! I have also come to love and appreciate my husband dearly.

God also said to me I have commanded you as a woman to be submissive and to love your husband. (*Ephesian 5:21-32-by submission I do not mean accepting abuse*) By not doing so you are in fact been disobedient to God's word as a Christian. I immediately repented and asked God for forgiveness. I began to obey the lord in my marriage. I change the way I think. I began to think of things that are good. I invested in my though. The way you think will either make you or destroy you. Think of good things for your husband or wife, pray for them with good intentions, not that they might go to bed one night and not get up so you can have the chance to pick up someone else. You have to understand that 3rd john 2 says it is the will of God for you to prosper in all your ways that includes your marriage.

It is different when you are single from when you are in a marriage. As a woman, you can be the young, single, independent, strong career woman you want when you are single, but when you get marriage you ought to add cooperation to the package. This is instituted by God; there is nothing you can do about it. Men you can be strong, carefree, with the untouchable sport car, plus a mothers boy, but when you get marriage you ought to be the priest of that home, you are to love, provide, pray for your family cling to your wife, and love her into submission.

Marriage couple are to sow seeds of encouragement; and refuse to let the devil have the best of them. Remember you are not alone. Sometime, God want us to be strong and able to manage our home as a preparation for the outpouring of his blessings and to take leadership position outside our homes.

In 1Timothy 3 the bible give up an insight of how a leader in the church should be and one of them is that a leader should be 'the husband of one wife, ... He must manage his own family well and see that his children obey him with proper respect'.

My prayer is that; as you read this book you received the power to excel in your marriage, that God will bless your home and family and give you wisdom to deal with your entire household problem, in Jesus name.

Giving and sowing of seed

Giving is a principle that God has given to us in order to bless us. The bibles talk about giving in both old and New Testament. We give to get approval of God to bless us. The bible tells us that when we give it shall be given to us in good measure, press down shaken together and running over. In the book of Malachi chapter 3 the bible tells us to put God in test with our tithe and offering and see if he will not rain down his blessing on us. God challenges us to give our tithe and offering to prove him if he will not bless us. Your tithe is like a seed, if you do not release it, it will not grow. If you keep your tithe in your hand and fail to release it, God will not release his blessing on his hands for you.

There is a special blessing that comes with giving. The moment you give a gift to the lord it becomes holy. This is why God teaches us how to give so that we will not give in an unworthy manner and miss our blessing. When we give we should not become self-conscious of the thing we have given, we must let it die in order for it to bear seed in your life. Don't give to seek recognition from man. In Mathew 6:2 Jesus warns us about this type of giving.

By giving to get recognition from man you will not be recognise by God. Many a time's people have resentment in giving to the church because they think the pastor is going to eat their money. We must not refuse to give because of what we think our pastors are going to do with the money. We must give as a way of obedient to God. When we give to obey God, our seed becomes a holy thing. If a minister of God decides to use the Holy thing of God unworthily, they will have to answer to God.

Judas was tempted by the devil because of his own characters. He was chosen among the entire crown that followed Jesus as one of the twelve disciples. He hard and saw Jesus preached but he was too engaged with his selfish desire.

As in the case of Judas it means you can be born again yet if you choose to walk in selfishness you could lose eternity. It did not had to be Judas who was to betray Jesus, but Judas use to steel the holy things of God. He uses to help himself with the money given to him to run the ministry of Jesus. He served as treasurer for the Apostles which meant he carried the money bag. John tells us that he was also dishonest and that he often stole money out of the bag whenever he wanted it. *(John 12:1-6)*

It was therefore, too easy for the devil to get through him.

Another character of the disciples of Jesus was Peter; Peter was ready to die for Jesus. He even cut the ear of the first man who laid his hands on Jesus. The devil could not have got away in tempting Peter in that manner, so he chooses Judas the money lover. So don't be worry about your money. If a so call pastor or anybody else in the church decide to steal from the collection gathered in church from Gods people theses persons are only exposing themselves to the devil. They will surely reap what they sow.

Righteousness

Righteousness simply means to do the right thing and following the ways of God. God promises us that when we seek God and his righteousness all other things shall be added to us. Righteousness comes with blessing from God. It is a promise of God to man. So what are these righteous things that God talked about in the bible, what did God referred to as righteous and why do we as Christian need to be righteous?

Faith by righteousness

The bible tells us that faith is the righteousness of God. We are considered as a righteous person when we work in Faith. It is the right thing to do when we have Faith in God. When we have Faith in God for anything in life, God consider us as righteous. Faith is defined in Hebrew 11:1 as "Now faith is being sure of what we hope for and certain of what we do not see." Faith is our confidence that we will receive the things we hope for in life. The bible tells us in Hebrews that it is impossible to please God without Faith. We become born again because of Faith, we believe by faith that Jesus is the son of God; he came on earth over 2000 thousand years, died for our sins, and was ascend into heaven will come again to take us to his kingdom. As a believer in Christ we hope to go to heaven, it is our desired wish to go to heaven, but it is by faith that we are confident that there is a place call heaven and we will get there.

In a conversation with a man of God, he made a very important point about faith that I found very interesting. He said the devil is not after our money nor is he after our possessions, what he is after he said, is our faith. He said this is so because, if the devil succeeded in taking our faith in Jesus then, the devil has succeeded in destroying our life. Cause without our faith in Jesus we are dead. Furthermore, he said, that is the reason why Jesus before he died prayed for Peter that his Faith will not fail. *"Simon, Simon, Satan has asked to sift you as wheat. But I have prayed for you Simon that your **Faith** may not fail. And when you have turned back, strengthen your brothers.* "Luke 22:31-32.

The bible tells us that it was accounted to Abram as righteousness because of his faith (Rom 3:3). God credited righteousness to Abraham and make him the father of all nation.

Always a reward comes when we work by Faith. Abram was living in his father's land were they did not believe in God; but by faith when God spoke to him to leave his father's land to a place that he will inherit, He obeyed God and went; even though he did not know where he was going. The bibles tell us in Hebrew 11 that, God considered him righteous because of his Faith to act.

In Hebrews 11:7 the bible tells us that Noah becomes heir of righteousness because of his faith. He believe that there was going to be a flood when he was warned by God even thought he had not seen it yet, and build a ark to save his family. So Faith brings righteousness, and one that is treasured by God.

Righteousness—by treating others right.

In Matthew 25:37-46 Jesus spoke of righteous as those who treat others right. The bible tells us when we feed others who are in need of feeding we are seen as a righteous person by God. This does not only mean the giving of food to the poor or charities but also to your brother who is in need. For example, if you know that your brother or sister has just lost his job and is in need for an immediate action to feed his or her family, you don't just say, I will pray for you, when you have what it takes to meet your brothers need. You simply give. By giving you will be credited righteousness by God. For any time you give to man for the sack of God, God will reward you. James1:27 "Religion that God our Father accepts as pure and faultless is this: to look after orphans and widows in their distress and to keep oneself from being polluted by the world."

You are to also look after the sick. Don't rejoice over an illness of another person, but rather be the one who will give support and kindness to the sick. Being greedy is a sin. There are people who just want in themselves. Everything about them is about me, me and me. They hurt others in expenses of their greediness and are jealous of the success of others. They are always comparing themselves with others and there life is full of negative behaviours. They are chasing everything they can and their love for money leads them into doing evil.

These people feel threaten to a stranger and instead of giving support they will spread there wigs to protect their territory.

When you became born again, your attitude should reflex Jesus, you have to lay down all those things that you use to do that do not glorify God or you know that Jesus will not do.

When you become a born again Christian, you choose to be different, people around you are watching you to see if indeed you are what you claim to be. In fact they expect you to be superman/woman. What other people will get away with you will not. One practical way to improve your attitude is to begin to pray and study the bible. As you read the word of God you mind and perception will change, this will eventually reflex on the outside.

The word of God will become alive in you, you should also get involved with other Christians and see how they do things; make a conscious effort to be like Jesus. You are to be honest and one who makes right judgement. You are not to judge wrongly or treat people in discrimination. John 7:24 tells us that we must stop judging by mere appearances and make right judgment.

In the New Testament Jesus commanded us that, we should love our God with all our heart and with all our might, to love our neighbour as we love ourselves. Our neighbours referred to as all those people whom we come across with in our normal life, to include people at work, home friends and family. This is the righteousness of God.

Righteousness and immorality

In my years of bible study and personal evangelism, this is the most famous of all. Whenever, righteousness is mention, the first thing that comes to people mind is immorality. Immorality is consider as unrighteousness in the bible. We will talk about sexual immorality as this is a sin that can permanently affect ones Christian growth unless completely abstain from it.

The bible tells us in 1Corinthians 6:13 that just, as food is for the stomach and stomach is for food so is our body for the lord. The bible tells us that our body was never meant for sexual immorality, but has been made for the Lord. In verse 15,1Corinthains 6, it tells us that as believer in Christ our bodies are members of Christ.

We cannot then take the body of Christ and united it with prostitute (this include pornography) by doing so you become one with the prostitute. Likewise, when we unite ourselves with the lord, we become one with him in spirit. God does not condemn the prostitute; He loves us all and died on the cross for all but when you receive Jesus, we must not go back to the old sin. The grace of God is also available for the repentant Christian.

The bible further tells us that our body is the temple of God. It is the place where the Holy Spirit lives. When we become born-again, we become the property of Jesus because; we were bought with a price, which is the incorruptible and precious blood of Jesus. This is why we are to honour God with our body. Sexual immorality drives the spirit of God from you. In verse 18, the bible tells us that it is the only sin that can cause one to sin against their own body. All other sin is committed outside our body and cannot affect us like the sin of sexual immorality.

When we allow the Holy Spirit of God to depart from us through sexual immorality, we became empty and powerless. We give space to the devil and create access for the devil in our life. Our Christian life will deteriorate. When David sin against God with Bathsheba, through sexual immorality; the bible tells us that the Holy Spirit left

David. In palm 51 David cried unto the Lord, he said, "Create in me a clean heart o lord and renew a right spirit within me, restore unto me the joy of your salvation." There is a certain joy, which fills your heart when the Holy Spirit is in you. The joy comes with your salvation when you first gave your life to the Lord. The spirit of God gives you a clean heart, a heart that will empower you to love beyond human understand and operate in the supernatural nature of God.

In Romans 6:12-14 the bible encourages us not to allow sin to reign in our body so that we do not obey its evil desires. However, we are to offer all the parts of our body to God as instruments of righteousness. God gave us the grace to overcome sin. When we work in the love of God we are working in his grace, and the love of God in us will empower us to work under his grace and we will be accounted as righteous.

God has promised us that when we live our life righteously, he will add to our life all other things we might need in life. So do not be jealous of people who live their life promiscuously. Your enjoyment should be in the things of God. Remember you are working into eternity.

If you have fallen into temptation and have sin against your body, do not stay there and start feeling sorry for yourself. Come out from it! Jesus died for your sins so that he might reposition you back to the lord. This is the perfect grace and love of God. If you confess your sins to the lord and call on his name, he will hear you and will take all your sins away and make you a new person.

God has promise never to leave us or, to forsake us, as long as you have life, use the opportunity and make up your mind to change. He is with you even in your last minute of your dying days. You might have driven him out of your life, but he is at the corner waiting for you to come back. He wants to help the backsliding Christian to become fully complete again. God loves us dearly; he loves our children more than we love them and cares about our wellbeing.

There is nothing that can separate us from the love of God, nothing, by any means can stop God from loving us. God has loved us with an everlasting love but he has given us the will to choose what we want. **What is your Choice?**

I agree that wealth is good and money can certainly buy you anything money can purchase. Nevertheless, it has limitations. Money cannot buy you eternal life nor can it purchase you death that you may live. So let reason together, "What shall it profit a man if he gains the whole world and loses his soul" Mark 8:36.

"The fool says in his heart there is no God" Psalm 14:1

THINK! DO YOU HAVE JESUS?

For more information on the way to eternal life, please contact me on the contact page you will find in this book. Your salvation is my concern. God bless you, in Jesus name! Amen

Zulibe Turner is an ordained Minister of the Gospel. She was publicly ordained in Reading UK as a DEACON by Bishop Ebi Edwards—Inatimi of The New Life International Worship Centre United Kingdom. She is also the Executive Director of Zunox Ltd register in England and wales.

She studies in England during which time she received her qualifications in Travel and Tourism Management.

Zulibe Turner as a teenager attended Freetown Bible Training Centre Sierra Leone marked 'the Joshua Generation' and was elected and serves in the National Scripture Union Leadership Team a.k.a Scripture Union Central Meeting.

Presently, Zulibe Turner lives in England and happily married with 2 beautiful children and worship at the Christ Abundant Life Ministry UK—Reading Branch.